MINITAB Guide
to Accompany
Introduction to the Practice
of Statistics

Second Edition

Betsy S. Greenberg
Mark A. Serva

The University of Texas at Austin

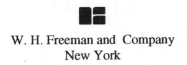

W. H. Freeman and Company
New York

MINITAB® is a registered trademark of Minitab, Inc. Output from MINITAB
is printed with permission of Minitab, Inc., State College, PA.

Cover Illustration by Salem Krieger

Printed in the United States of America

ISBN: 0-7167-2483-9

Third printing 1995, RRD

Table of Contents

Preface

This *Minitab Guide* accompanies the Second Edition of *Introduction to the Practice of Statistics* by David S. Moore and George P. McCabe and is intended to be used with the statistical software package called Minitab. Minitab was originally developed twenty years ago for students in introductory statistics courses. Using Minitab relieves students of tedious statistical calculations and allows them to better understand statistical concepts.

Minitab is available on a wide variety of computers, including mainframes and personal computers. For further information about the system, contact

> Minitab, Inc.
> 3081 Enterprise Drive
> State College, PA 16801-2756
> 814-238-3280

An inexpensive student version, The Student Edition of MINITAB, is available for Macintosh, IBM, and IBM compatible computers from Addison-Wesley.

This *Minitab Guide* parallels the Second Edition of *Introduction to the Practice of Statistics* by David S. Moore and George P. McCabe. In this supplement we refer to the textbook as *I.P.S.* The *Minitab Guide* contains an introduction to Minitab plus a chapter corresponding to each chapter in *I.P.S.* In each chapter, we show how Minitab can be used to perform the statistical techniques described in *I.P.S.* In addition, each chapter includes exercises selected and modified from *I.P.S.* that are appropriate to be done using Minitab. The numbering of the exercises refers to exercises in *I.P.S.* The Appendix lists by topic Minitab commands and subcommands that are referred to in this supplement. A data disks that contains the Minitab worksheets used in this supplement is available for instructors.

Acknowledgments

Software was provided to the authors through Minitab Inc.'s author assistance program. Hardware was provided by Project QUEST at The University of Texas at Austin.

We are grateful to the many individuals who helped with the preparation of this supplement. Anonymous reviewers, John Butler, Matt Kammer-Kerwick, Hongmin Lu, David Moore, Yun Song, and Neerja Wadhwa all provided helpful comments and suggestions. Mary Parker tested an earlier version of this supplement in her classes at Austin Community College. Martha Smith provided secretarial assistance. Wade Odell provided support and encouragement.

Introduction to Minitab

Commands to be covered in this chapter:

```
STOP session
SET the following data into C
END of data
INFOrmation [on C,...,C] on status of worksheet
HELP [command]
SAVE [in 'FILENAME'] a copy of the worksheet
READ the following data into C,...,C
NAME C is 'NAME', C is 'NAME',...,C is 'NAME'
RETRieve the saved Minitab worksheet from 'FILENAME'
PRINt E,...,E
INSErt data [between rows K and K] of C,...,C
DELEte rows K,...,K of C,...,C
LET C(K) = K
ERASe E,...,E
OUTFile 'FILENAME'
NOOUtfile
```

What Minitab Will Do for You

Before the widespread availability of powerful computers and prepackaged statistics programs, manual computations were emphasized in statistics courses. Today, computers have revolutionized data analysis, which is a fundamental task of statistics. Packages such as Minitab allow the computer to solve statistics problems. Minitab can perform a wide variety of tasks from the construction of graphical and numerical summaries for a set of data to the complicated statistical procedures and tests described in the book Second Edition of *Introduction to the Practice of Statistics* by David S. Moore and George P. McCabe. In this supplement, we will refer to the textbook as *I.P.S.* The numbering of exercises refers to exercises in *I.P.S.*

For the student, Minitab will allow you to concentrate less on the mathematical calculations and more on the analysis of the data. As with learning any computer package,

1

there is a considerable time investment required. We recommend that you reserve several hours in the beginning to get a feel for what Minitab can do. Of course, if you have never used a computer before, allow yourself even more time. After the initial time investment, Minitab will allow you to take advantage of the power of statistical computation.

Beginning and Ending a Minitab Session

To start a Minitab session, type MINITAB at the prompt for your computer system. Different computer systems will have different prompts. Examples of system prompts are $ and A>. For Macintosh systems, double click on the Minitab system icon. Once you have entered Minitab, the prompt will be MTB >.

The STOP Command

To end a Minitab session and exit the program, type STOP at the Minitab prompt (MTB >).

The Minitab Worksheet

The worksheet is arranged by rows and columns. The columns, C1, C2, C3,..., correspond to the variables in your data, the rows to observations. In addition, the worksheet may also include stored constants, K1, K2, K3,..., as illustrated below.

The Minitab Worksheet

	C1	C2	C3	C4	. . .	C1000
1						
2						
3						
.						
.						
.						

K1	K2	K3	. . .		

The above worksheet shows one thousand addressable columns. In practice, the number of columns and rows will depend on the machine and the system on which Minitab is implemented.

Columns

Most of the Minitab commands address the columns. In general, a column contains data for one variable, and each row contains all the data for each subject or observation. Columns can be referred to by number (C1, C2, C3,...) or by names such as 'height' or 'weight'. Names are assigned to columns using the **NAME** command, which is described later in this chapter.

Constants

Constants are referenced by the letter "K" and a number (K1, K2, K3,...). Unlike columns, constants are single values. Storing a constant tells Minitab to remember this value: it will be needed later. Constants are analogous to the memory functions on most calculators. For instance, Minitab allows you to quickly find the average of a column of one hundred numbers. Instead of having to write it down, the value can be stored into a constant such as K1 and used in subsequent calculations.

Minitab Commands

Commands tell Minitab what to do. For example, the **STOP** command, described above, tells Minitab to end a session. Commands are entered at the Minitab prompt (MTB >). If you are using a Macintosh, IBM, or IBM compatible computer, you can also use menu commands. Menu commands correspond closely with session commands. When you execute a menu command, Minitab displays the corresponding session commands. We describe session commands in this book because a Minitab user on *any* computer can use them.

Commands always start with a command word, such as **SET**. Only the first four letters of a command word are needed. A command may require more data, such as the column(s) or constant(s) on which the action is performed. Additional letters and text may be added for clarity. For the remainder of this book, only the required letters will be capitalized when discussing or explaining a command. The remainder of the command word and any extra text used to help explain commands are written in lowercase. Minitab accepts either upper- or lowercase and does not distinguish between them. In the examples in this book, commands are in lower case.

Command syntax is described in this book using special symbols, for example C, K, E, FILENAME, and square brackets. When you use a command, replace C by a specific column, using either the number (e.g., C2) or name, enclosed in single quotes (e.g., 'HEIGHT'). Replace K by a number (e.g., 5.2) or a stored constant (e.g., K4). Replace E by either a column, a number, or a stored constant. Some commands have optional arguments. When the syntax for these commands is given, the optional arguments are enclosed in square brackets. Some commands may refer to files. To use these, replace FILENAME by a specific file name, enclosed in single quotes.

Both column names and file names are enclosed in single quotes. Some computer keyboareds have both right (´) and left (`) single quotes. The right quote must be used; the left quote is not recognized in Minitab.

The SET Command*

The **SET** command is used to enter data into a Minitab worksheet one column at a time. The format for the command is as follows:

```
SET the following data into C
```

where C designates a single column, for example, C1. After entering the **SET** command, Minitab expects data and returns the data prompt (DATA>). Entered numbers may be separated with either spaces or commas. Each time the return key is used, Minitab will return the data prompt. The command **END** signifies that the data for the column are complete. Minitab will discontinue the data prompt and return to the Minitab prompt. Another **SET** command could also be used to tell Minitab that the data for one column are complete and that you will then be entering data for another column.

In the following example, the number of home runs that Babe Ruth hit in each of his years with the New York Yankees is entered into column C1. These data could be entered into Minitab several different ways. The data may be entered all on one line, two or more lines, separated by spaces or commas, or even with one number on each line. The command can be entered in upper- or lowercase and the user can enter additional words if desired. Four methods are illustrated below:

Examples:

1)
```
MTB > set c1
DATA> 54 59 35 41 46 25 47 60 54 46 49 46 41 34 22
DATA> end
```

2)
```
MTB > set all of the data in c1
DATA> 54 59 35 41 46 25 47
DATA> 60 54 46 49 46 41 34 22
DATA> end
```

3)
```
MTB > SET C1
DATA> 54,59,35,41,46,25,47,60,54,46,49,46,41,34,22
DATA> END
```

---

* If you are using a Macintosh, IBM, or IBM compatible computer, data can be entered with the Data window. If you are using an IBM or compatible computer, you can use either the Edit menu or Alt+D and Alt+M to go back and forth between the Data window and the Session window. If you are using a Macintosh computer, you can use either the Window menu or ⌘+D and ⌘+M to go back and forth between the Data and Session windows. If you are using the Data window, the commands **SET** and **READ** may be less useful, however; they are still available.

4)
```
MTB > set c1
DATA> 54
DATA> 59
DATA> 35
DATA> 41
DATA> 46
DATA> 25
DATA> 47
DATA> 60
DATA> 54
DATA> 46
DATA> 49
DATA> 46
DATA> 41
DATA> 34
DATA> 22
DATA> end
```

After entering the above data, the Minitab worksheet will appear as illustrated below.

The Minitab Worksheet

	C1	C2	C3	C4	. . .	C1000
1	54					
2	59					
3	35					
4	41					
5	46					
6	25					
7	47					
8	60					
9	54					
10	46					
11	49					
12	46					
13	41					
14	34					
15	22					
.						
.						
.						

K1	K2	K3	. . .		

The `INFOrmation` Command

The `INFOrmation` command is used to list the contents of the current Minitab worksheet. Note that we present this command by capitalizing only the essential four letters, while still spelling out the entire word. The format for the `INFOrmation` command is

```
INFOrmation [on C,...,C] on status of worksheet
```

For the `INFOrmation` command, specifying columns is optional, as indicated by the square brackets. If no columns are specified, `INFOrmation` lists the attributes of all columns and constants. For example, for the current worksheet with 15 observation in C1, the `INFOrmation` command would display the following information:

```
MTB > info

COLUMN      NAME      COUNT
C1                     15

CONSTANTS USED: NONE
```

The output generated above reveals that there are currently fifteen data elements or observations in column C1. No other columns or constants contain any data. If one or more columns are specified with the `INFOrmation` command, then Minitab will supply information about only those columns.

```
MTB > info c1

COLUMN      NAME      COUNT
C1                     15
```

Extra text may be added to Minitab commands. In the following example, the letters "on the column" are added to increase the clarity of the command.

```
MTB > info on the column c1

COLUMN      NAME      COUNT
C1                     15
```

The `HELP` Command

Minitab has an extensive help library available to explain commands. Commands are explained in `HELP` using the same conventions as in the book. The format for the `HELP` command is

```
HELP [command]
```

For example, help is obtained for the `INFOrmation` command below.

```
MTB > help info

INFORMATION [on C,...,C] on status of worksheet

If no columns are specified, INFO prints a list of all
columns used with their names and counts, all stored
constants used, and all matrices used.  If you list
columns, the information on just these columns is given.
```

Help is even available for the **HELP** command by typing HELP HELP. The **HELP** command can assist users in becoming adept at Minitab. In fact, **HELP** can be consulted before referencing this handbook. The on-line help is concise and at a user's fingertips. The **HELP** command should be used often to increase Minitab's effectiveness.

To get a list of the Minitab commands in one of the categories below, type HELP COMMANDS followed by the appropriate number.[*]

1	General Information	11	Tables
2	Input and Output of Data	12	Time Series
3	Editing and Manipulating	13	Statistical Process Control
	Data	14	Exploratory Data Analysis
4	Arithmetic	15	Distributions and Random Data
5	Plotting Data	16	Sorting
6	Basic Statistics	17	Matrices
7	Regression	18	Miscellaneous
8	Analysis of Variance	19	Stored Commands and Loops
9	Multivariate Analysis	20	How Commands Are Explained
10	Nonparametrics		in HELP

Below, we illustrate **HELP** using category 2 to obtain a list of commands for entering data.

```
MTB > help commands 2

COMMANDS 2. Input and Output of Data

    READ         (enter data from terminal or data file)
    SET          (enter data from terminal or data file)
    INSERT       (enter data from terminal or data file)
    END          (end input entered with READ, SET, INSERT, and STORE)
    RETRIEVE     (enter data from a saved worksheet file)
    NAME         (name columns)
    PRINT        (view data on the screen)
    WRITE        (output data to screen or data file)
    SAVE         (output data to a saved worksheet file)
```

---

[*] If you are using a Macintosh, IBM, or IBM compatible computer, the topics are available from a menu once you have used the **HELP** command.

The SAVE Command

The **SAVE** command allows the data in a worksheet to be stored so that it can be used later. If there is a chance that a worksheet will be needed in the future, it is better to **SAVE** the data to a file than to retype it. The format for the **SAVE** command is

```
SAVE [in 'FILENAME'] a copy of the worksheet
```

If Minitab is used on a personal computer, it is recommended to have one disk solely for projects and homework problems from the text. Filenames should reflect the work performed on the data set. Using problem names, such as 'Prob2-21', works well, as does a descriptive name such as 'Ruth'. Using periods (.) or colons (:) is not recommended in any Minitab filename. A hyphen (-), an underline (_), or even a blank space can be used instead. To save Babe Ruth's home run data, use the **SAVE** command as follows:

```
MTB > save 'BABE'

Worksheet saved into file: BABE.MTW
```

The file BABE.MTW will contain the data {54, 59, 35, 41, 46, 25, 47, 60, 54, 46, 49, 46, 41, 34, 22} that were entered into column C1 using the **SET** command. Minitab uses the filename extension MTW to indicate that a file is a Minitab worksheet. The filename extension MTW should *not* be entered as part of the filename, because Minitab will add it automatically whenever the **SAVE** command is used. The number of characters allowed for filenames depends on the kind of computer that is being used.

The READ Command

The **READ** command is commonly used to enter more than one column of data at a time. For the **READ** command, all of the columns have to be of the same length. The command format is as follows:

```
READ the following data into C,...,C
```

To illustrate the **READ** command, suppose that an instructor wants to enter into Minitab test scores from a midterm and a final examination. The test data will be entered as follows: the student identification numbers will be entered into C1; the midterm exam scores will be entered into C2; and the final exam scores into C3. The following data are for five of the students in the class.

Student ID#	Midterm Exam	Final Exam
11111	85	92
23456	72	78
33344	77	79
41414	92	90
52525	90	85

The data can be entered using either the **SET** or the **READ** command. If the **SET** command is used, the data must be entered one column at a time:

```
MTB > set c1
DATA> 11111 23456 33344 41414 52525
MTB > set c2
DATA> 85 72 77 92 90
MTB > set c3
DATA> 92 78 79 90 85
DATA> end
```

If the **READ** command is used, however, all three columns can be entered at the same time as illustrated below.

```
MTB > read c1 c2 c3
DATA> 11111 85 92
DATA> 23456 72 78
DATA> 33344 77 79
DATA> 41414 92 90
DATA> 52525 90 85
DATA> end
      5 ROWS READ
```

The Minitab worksheet now will contain three columns of data:

```
MTB > info

COLUMN    NAME      COUNT
C1                    5
C2                    5
C3                    5

CONSTANTS USED: NONE
```

The **READ** command can also be used to import data from a text file. The format in this case is

```
READ data from 'FILENAME' into C,...,C
```

The NAME Command

Minitab allows us to name columns. If a column is named, it may be referenced by its name. It's often easier to remember the name of a variable than the number of a column. In addition, all output will then be labeled with the name, making the output easier to interpret. The format for the NAME command is

```
NAME C is 'NAME', C is 'NAME',..., C is 'NAME'
```

For example, if we want to name the columns in our current worksheet, we might use the names illustrated below.

```
MTB > name c1 'IDs' c2 'midterm' c3 'final'
MTB > info

COLUMN      NAME        COUNT
C1          IDs           5
C2          midterm       5
C3          final         5

CONSTANTS USED: NONE
```

These names now can substitute for the column number in any command. For instance, if information about column C3, the final examination, is desired, we can use the name 'final' as illustrated below.

```
MTB > info 'final'

COLUMN      NAME        COUNT
C3          final          5
```

The above command will generate the same results as

```
MTB > info c3

COLUMN      NAME        COUNT
C3          final          5
```

Whenever a column name is used in a command, it must be enclosed in single quotes. Names may be up to eight characters and can use any character except the pound sign (#) and the single quote ('). Names can be changed simply by using the NAME command on the same column a second time. If a list of current names is desired, the INFO command will list all current columns and any associated names. Minitab does not differentiate between uppercase and lowercase letters in names: 'IDS' is equivalent to 'IDs'. However, Minitab will print the name in upper- and lowercase as it was entered in the NAME command.

The RETRieve Command

Whenever the **READ** or **SET** commands are used on a column that contains data, the original data will be erased and the new data will be assigned to the column. When the **READ** command was used to enter the data in the above example, Babe Ruth's home run data were erased from the current worksheet.

However, the home run data have not been lost, because the **SAVE** command was used before the test data were entered. To recall the data from the BABE.MTW file, the **RETRieve** command is used. The **RETRieve** command loads into Minitab worksheet files that have been previously saved using the **SAVE** command. The format for the **RETRieve** command is

```
RETRIEVE the saved Minitab worksheet from 'FILENAME'
```

The **RETRieve** command will also erase the entire contents of the current worksheet before loading the file. So that the test data are not lost, use the **SAVE** command to save the data set:

```
MTB > save 'TEST'

Worksheet saved into file: TEST.MTW
```

To recall the home run data set, use the **RETRieve** command as follows:

```
MTB > retr 'babe'
 WORKSHEET SAVED  7/ 6/1991

Worksheet retrieved from file: BABE.MTW
```

To verify that the test data are no longer on the current worksheet, use the **INFOrmation** command:

```
MTB > info

COLUMN     NAME       COUNT
C1                       15

CONSTANTS USED: NONE
```

The only column that contains data is now C1. All other columns have been erased.

The PRINt Command

The **PRINt** command displays data contained in the worksheet on your screen. **PRINt** will display the values contained in either columns or constants. The format for the command is

```
PRINt E,...,E
```

Before demonstrating the **PRINt** command, we will name the data in C1.

```
MTB > name c1 'ruth'
MTB > print c1

ruth
    54    59    35    41    46    25    47    60    54    46    49
    46    41    34    22
```

If only one column is specified, the data will be displayed horizontally, without row numbers. Minitab will print the data with row numbers only if more than one column is specified. If only one column is to be printed and row numbers are required, specify the desired column (C1) and an empty column, such as C20.

```
MTB > print c1 c20

    ROW    ruth    C20

      1      54
      2      59
      3      35
      4      41
      5      46
      6      25
      7      47
      8      60
      9      54
     10      46
     11      49
     12      46
     13      41
     14      34
     15      22
```

Changing the Data

Minitab provides four commands to change the values in the data set: **INSErt**, **DELEte**, **LET**, and **ERASe**. The **INSErt** command allows rows to be added at the beginning, middle, or end of a column. The **DELEte** command will remove data items from columns. The **LET** command can be used to change individual data elements. The **ERASe** command is used to remove constants or entire columns from the data set. We will illustrate these commands using the data contained in TEST.MTW. The **RETRieve** command can be used so that this worksheet can be used again.

```
MTB > retr 'test'
 WORKSHEET SAVED  1/19/1992

Worksheet retrieved from file: TEST.MTW
```

The INSErt Command

The **INSErt** command is used to add data at the top, between two rows, or at the bottom of columns of data.   Data cannot be added to a column or group of columns using the **SET** or **READ** commands. These commands will erase the original data and replace them with new data. The format for the **INSErt** command is

```
INSErt data [between rows K and K] of C,...,C
```

The columns C,...,C designate the columns on which to perform the insertion. The constant values K and K specify between which two rows the data are to be inserted. If no rows are specified, then the data are appended to the ends of the columns.

To insert data at the beginning of a column, the rows 0 and 1 are specified. For instance, suppose that in the student test data set, two students were allowed to take makeup examinations and were not included in the original Minitab worksheet. Their student ID numbers are 01010 and 01234. The first student scored a 91 on the midterm and an 85 on the final. The second student scored an 82 and an 89. Because the test scores are listed in order by student ID number and these students' ID numbers are the first and second numbers in the class, their test scores must be inserted at the top of the worksheet. Instead of retyping the entire worksheet, use the **INSErt** command as follows:

```
MTB > insert between rows 0 and 1 for columns c1 c2 c3
DATA> 01010 91 85
DATA> 01234 82 89
DATA> end
      2 ROWS READ
```

The worksheet will now contain the following data. The new columns are boxed. Note that leading zeros do not appear.

ROW	IDs	midterm	final
1	1010	91	85
2	1234	82	89
3	11111	85	92
4	23456	72	78
5	33344	77	79
6	41414	92	90
7	52525	90	85

To insert data in the middle of the columns, use the row numbers between which you want to insert the data. To insert data for student ID numbers 24242 and 27772 into the worksheet, use the following command:

```
MTB > insert 4 5 c1-c3
DATA> 24242 90 81
DATA> 27772 71 80
DATA> end
      2 ROWS READ
```

The data were inserted between rows 4 and 5 to maintain the numerical ordering of the student ID numbers. The hyphen (-) specifies that the data are to be inserted into columns C1, C2, and C3. The same command could be entered by typing

```
MTB >  insert 4 5 c1 c2 c3
```

The modified worksheet is shown below. Once again, the new columns are boxed. Notice that the new data have been inserted after row 4 and before the old row 5. After the insertion, the old row 5 becomes row 7.

```
MTB > print c1-c3

ROW      IDs  midterm    final

  1     1010       91       85
  2     1234       82       89
  3    11111       85       92
  4    23456       72       78
  5    24242       90       81
  6    27772       71       80
  7    33344       77       79
  8    41414       92       90
  9    52525       90       85
```

Another common use of the **INSErt** command is the appending of data to the end of a column. To append data to the end of a column, specify only the columns to which you want to append; do not specify any row numbers. For example, to append the test scores 95 and 91 for student number 99999 to the end of columns C1 through C3:

```
MTB > insert c1-c3
DATA> 99999 95 91
DATA> end
     1 ROWS READ
```

Since no row is specified, Minitab assumes you want the data appended to columns C1 through C3. Columns 1, 2, and 3 now contain the following data:

```
MTB > print c1-c3

ROW      IDs  midterm    final

  1     1010       91       85
  2     1234       82       89
  3    11111       85       92
  4    23456       72       78
  5    24242       90       81
  6    27772       71       80
  7    33344       77       79
  8    41414       92       90
  9    52525       90       85
 10    99999       95       91
```

The DELEte Command

The DELEte command removes unwanted data from columns. The format for the command is:

```
DELEte rows K,...,K of C,...,C
```

The constant values K,...,K designate which row numbers to delete. The columns C,...,C determine on which column to perform the operation. Using the 'new-test' data set, if the student corresponding to row 6 drops the course, we can remove his test scores from the data set by using the DELEte command as follows:

```
MTB > delete row 6 from columns c1 c2 c3
```

Minitab removes the items in row 6 from columns 1, 2, and 3. The worksheet now contains the following data:

```
ROW    IDs  midterm  final

  1    1010    91     85
  2    1234    82     89
  3   11111    85     92
  4   23456    72     78
  5   24242    90     81
  6   33344    77     79
  7   41414    92     90
  8   52525    90     85
  9   99999    95     91
```

To remove more than one consecutive row, a colon is used to designate the interval. To remove nonconsecutive rows, list the row numbers, separated by spaces or commas.

Examples:

```
MTB > delete 2 4 c2 c3
```
(Will delete rows 2 and 4 from columns 2 and 3)

```
MTB > delete 2:4 c2
```
(Will delete rows 2, 3, and 4 from column 2)

```
MTB > delete 3:6 c5 c8
```
(Will delete rows 3, 4, 5, and 6 from columns 5 and 8)

As with any command that removes data from the worksheet, the SAVE command should be used before the DELEte command. If the row or column numbers are misjudged, the data can be retrieved and the operation can be performed again.

The LET Command

The **LET** command can be used to change a single observation in a column. It is commonly used to correct data entry errors. According to the student data set, student 23456 scored a 78 on the final exam:

```
ROW     IDs  midterm   final

  1     1010     91      85
  2     1234     82      89
  3    11111     85      92
  4    23456     72      78
  5    24242     90      81
  6    33344     77      79
  7    41414     92      90
  8    52525     90      85
  9    99999     95      91
```

Because the teaching assistant graded her final exam incorrectly, her score should have been an 87. Instead of reentering the entire column, the **LET** command allows a single observation to be changed:

```
MTB > let c3(4) = 87
```

The observation in the fourth row in C3 is denoted by C3(4). The **LET** command replaces 78 with the new value of 87. Note: You cannot reverse the order; for example, LET 87 = C3(4) will not work.

The ERASe Command

The **ERASe** command can be used to remove columns or constants that you no longer need. The format for the command is

```
ERASe E,...,E
```

For example, the midterm examination data in the second column can be erased from the worksheet as follows:

```
MTB > erase c2
MTB > info

COLUMN      NAME        COUNT
C1          IDs             9
C3          final           9

CONSTANTS USED: NONE
```

The OUTFile Command

The OUTFile command is used to create a log of the commands that have been used and the output that has been generated for a work session. The contents are sent to a designated file. The command format is

```
OUTFile 'FILENAME'
```

The OUTFile command will not save any of the data that have been entered or generated. It will only save what is typed or printed to the screen in a work session. To stop sending output to the file, use the command NOOUtfile. For example, enter the following commands into Minitab:

```
MTB > outfile 'diary'
MTB > set c1
DATA> 11.5 3.0 11.7 13.9 10.3
DATA> end
MTB > print c1

C1
    11.5     3.0    11.7    13.9    10.3

MTB > nooutfile
```

Just as Minitab uses the filename extension MTW to designate worksheet files, Minitab automatically adds the filename extension LIS to keep track of listings. The extension LIS should not be included in the filename: Minitab will add it automatically. A text file DIARY.LIS will be created that contains the following information:

```
MTB > set c1
MTB > end
MTB > print c1

C1
    11.5     3.0    11.7    13.9    10.3

MTB > nooutfile
```

Note that the data entry lines from the SET command have not been included in the output. When using the OUTFile command, Minitab will only keep track of the commands and the output, not the data.

One convention that works well when choosing a filename is to use the homework name and number for the outfile name—HMWRK1—and the problem number when saving the data—PRB2-21.

An effective use of the OUTFile command is to record the procedures followed when completing a homework assignment. By sending the file to the printer, you will have a hard copy of the exact commands you used and the output that they generated.

If the same name is used with the `OUTFile` command as was used previously, Minitab will either create a new listing file with this name or append the additional output to the existing file. Which actually occurs will depend on the computer system being used.

Worksheet files are coded with special symbols that only Minitab can read: they cannot be printed out or edited. Since outfiles are text files, however, they can be edited by most word processors and can be sent to a printer. Understanding the difference between outfiles and worksheet files is an important but often confusing topic with students who are learning Minitab. When the `OUTFile` command is entered into Minitab, it will immediately start sending whatever is printed out to the screen to a file that the user designates. Minitab will automatically add the filename extension LIS to the filename. Minitab will not send the contents of the worksheet to the file: the user must execute the `SAVE` command to ensure that the contents of the Minitab worksheet will be saved to a designated file. Minitab will automatically add the filename extension MTW to any file saved under the `SAVE` command.

The `RETRieve` command is used to recall files that have been saved with the `SAVE` command. `RETRieve` will also erase all contents of the Minitab worksheet before the file data are recalled. Outfiles cannot be retrieved into Minitab, but can be printed out on a printer.

EXERCISES

1. Use the `OUTFile` command to start a record of your work. Use the name 'HW_CH0'.

2. Use the `SET` command to enter these crankshaft data into column 1:

224.120	223.960	224.098	223.001	224.089	224.057	224.017
223.987	223.913	223.982	223.976	223.999	223.989	223.902

3. Use the `INFOrmation` command to verify that 14 observations were entered. Use the `PRINt` command to verify that no data entry errors were made.

4. The fourth number listed above is 223.001, which is incorrect. Use the `LET` command to correct the data set so that the fourth number is 224.001.

5. Use the `NAME` command to name C1 'cranks'. Verify the name with the `INFOrmation` command.

6. Access and read the `HELP` information for the `INSErt` and `DELEte` commands.

7. Append the following observations to the data using the `INSErt` command. Use the name 'cranks' when referring to the data set.

223.961   223.980

Verify that the data have been appended to the end of the file using the **PRINt** command.

8.   Use the **SAVE** command to store the worksheet. Use the name 'EX111'. **RETRieve** the data and use the **INFOrmation** command or the **PRINt** command to ensure that the data and name for C1 are correctly entered.

9.   Close the listing file using the command **NOOUtfile**. Use the **STOP** command to leave Minitab. From the course instructor or the computation center, obtain the procedure for printing out files. Generate a hard copy of your work by printing the listing file, HW_CH0.LIS. Do not attempt to obtain a hard copy of the worksheet file, EX111.MTW.

10.   Create a Minitab worksheet called 'HOMERUN'. Name C1 'Ruth' and name C2 'Maris'. Enter the following home run data into the appropriate columns and verify that you have entered the data correctly.

Ruth	54	59	35	41	46	25	47	60	54	46	49	4	4	34	22
Maris	8	13	14	16	23	26	28	33	39	61					

Chapter 1
Looking at Data: Distributions

Commands to be covered in this chapter:

`STEM-and-leaf` display of C,...,C

`HISTogram` of C,...,C

`DOTPlot` of data in C,...,C

`STACk` (E,...,E) on ... on (E,...,E) put into (C,...,C)

`TSPLot` [period = K] time series data in C

`DESCribe` the data in C,...,C

`BOXPlot` for data in C

`LET` (algebraic expression, complete on one line)

`MEAN` of values in C [put mean into K]

`RMEAn` E,...,E put mean of each row into C

`CDF` for values in E [store results in E]

`NSCOres` of C, put into C

`PLOT` C vs C

`RANDom` K observations into each of C,...,C

Picturing Distributions

The distribution of a variable can be displayed graphically with Minitab commands such as `STEM-and-leaf`, `HISTogram`, and `DOTPlot`. Histograms and stemplots are useful to show the shape of a distribution. Both group the data into just a few intervals. Stemplots allow individual data points to be displayed. Dotplots divide the axis into more classes. Below we will illustrate these commands using the BABE.MTW data set that was used in the Introduction. You may simply retrieve this file or reenter the data as shown below.

The STEM-and-leaf Command

A stem-and-leaf plot uses the actual data to create the display. The format for the STEM-and-leaf command is

```
STEM-and-leaf display of C,...,C
```

The command is illustrated below on the Babe Ruth home run data set.

```
MTB > set c1
DATA> 54 59 35 41 46 25 47 60 54 46 49 46 41 34 22
DATA> end
MTB > name c1 'ruth'
MTB > stem c1

Stem-and-leaf of ruth      N  = 15
Leaf Unit = 1.0

    1      2 2
    2      2 5
    3      3 4
    4      3 5
    6      4 11
   (5)     4 66679
    4      5 44
    2      5 9
    1      6 0
```

The first column of a stem-and-leaf display is called the depth, the second column holds the stems, and the rest of the display holds the leaves. Each leaf digit represents one observation. In the above stemplot, the first stem is 2 and the first leaf is 2. The corresponding observation is 22. The leaf unit at the top of the display tells us where to put the decimal point. In the above example, the Leaf Unit = 1.0, so the decimal point goes at the end.

The first column, the depth, has one special line: the line that contains the median. Its value is enclosed in parentheses and says how many observations are on just that line. For the remaining lines, the depth gives a cumulative count from the top and bottom. For example, the number 6 on the fifth line from the top says there are six observations on that line and the four lines above. They are 22, 25, 34, 35, 41, and 41. The number 4 on the third line from the bottom says there are four observations on that line and below. The sixth stem represents the numbers 46, 46, 46, 47, and 49.

The HISTogram Command

While stem-and-leaf plots are useful for small sets of data, histograms are particularly useful for large data sets. Unlike the stem-and-leaf plot, histograms use the midpoint of a data range for scaling and represent an observation by the asterisk (*). The format for the HISTogram command is

```
HISTogram of C,...,C
```

Below we illustrate the use of the histogram on Babe Ruth's home run data.

```
MTB > hist c1

Histogram of ruth    N = 15

Midpoint   Count
      20       1   *
      25       1   *
      30       0
      35       2   **
      40       2   **
      45       4   ****
      50       1   *
      55       2   **
      60       2   **
```

Note that the shape of the distribution looks slightly different when displayed with the **HISTogram** command than it did with the **STEM-and-leaf** command. This is because the scaling is a bit different. For example, the third interval in the above histogram is 27.5 to 32.5 (with a midpoint at 30), while the third interval in the previous stem-and-leaf plot was 30 to 34. There are no observations between 27.5 and 32.5, but there is one observation (34) in the third interval of the stem-and-leaf display.

The **DOTPlot** Command

The display provided by the **DOTPlot** command is very similar to a histogram with a horizontal axis and many small intervals. Dotplots are also useful if you want to compare two or more sets of data. The format for the **DOTPlot** command is

```
DOTPlot of data in C,...,C
```

Again, we illustrate this command with the home run data.

```
MTB > dotplot 'ruth'
```

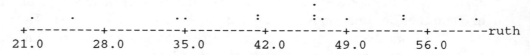

```
          .       .                    ..       :       :.  .       :           . .
         +---------+---------+---------+---------+---------+---------+-------ruth
         21.0      28.0      35.0      42.0      49.0      56.0
```

Notice that while the shapes for the stem-and-leaf plot and the histogram are similar, the dotplot appears more widely distributed. All three descriptive methods use different methods of grouping the data, so the distributions will look somewhat different.

Several columns of data can be specified with each of the commands **HISTogram**, **STEM-and-leaf**, and **DOTPlot**. An individual display will be printed for each column of data listed with the command. For example, we may examine the number of home runs hit by Roger Maris for each of his ten years in the American League.

```
MTB > set c1
DATA> 8 13 14 16 23 26 28 33 39 61
DATA> end
MTB > name c2 'maris'
MTB > dotp c1 c2
```

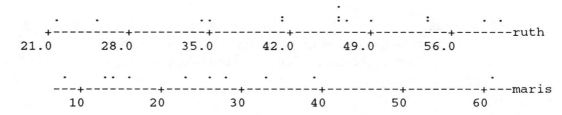

When comparing two or more distributions, the displays should be drawn on axes with the same range. This can be done using Minitab subcommands as described below.

Subcommands

Many commands have subcommands that provide Minitab with additional information. To use a subcommand, put a semicolon at the end of the main command line. This tells Minitab that subcommands will follow. Minitab will prompt the user with the SUBC> subcommand prompt. If more than one subcommand will be used, start each on a new line and end all except the last with a semicolon. End the last subcommand with a period.

Using **HELP** with a Minitab command name will produce a list of the available subcommands. For example, we see below that the subcommands **INCRement**, **STARt**, **BY**, and **SAME** can be used with the command **DOTPlot**. As with main Minitab command words, only the first four letters of a subcommand word are needed. Using **HELP** with the command name and the subcommand name will provide information about the subcommand.

```
MTB > help dotp
DOTPLOT of data in C,...,C

Subcommands:   INCREMENT   START   BY   SAME

MTB > help dotp same
SAME

Force all displays to be drawn on axes with the same (i.e. the largest)
range.
```

```
MTB > dotp c1 c2;
SUBC> same.
```

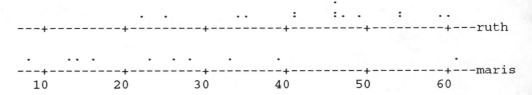

Displays on the same axes can also be obtained using the **STARt** and **INCRement** subcommands to specify the first plotting position and the distance between the tick marks on the axis. These subcommands can be used with one or more columns of data to specify the scale of the display.

```
MTB > dotp c1 c2;
SUBC> start 8;
SUBC> increment 12.
```

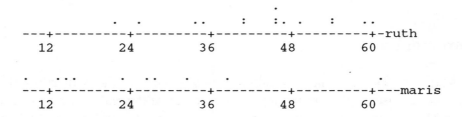

The **STACk** Command

A third way to produce displays on axes of the same length is with the **BY** subcommand. To use this subcommand, the data must be in a single column with identifying codes in another column. Data can be arranged in this way by using the **STACk** command with the following format.

```
STACk (E,...,E) on ... on (E,...,E) put into (C,...,C)
```

At least three columns must be specified when using the **STACk** command. Minitab will place the contents of the first column on top of the contents of the second column and place the result in the third column. The **SUBScripts** subcommand can be used to create a column of data that identifies to which column the data originally belonged before the **STACk** command was executed. The **SUBScripts** command format is

```
SUBScripts into C
```

In the following example, we will stack the data for both Babe Ruth and Roger Maris into C3. The **SUBScripts** subcommand will place codes into column C4 identifying the baseball player (Ruth = 1, Maris = 2). Once the data are arranged in this manner, we will use the **BY** subcommand with the **DOTPlot** command to obtain displays using the same axis.

```
MTB > stack 'ruth' on 'maris' put into c3;
SUBC> subscripts c4.
MTB > name c3 'homeruns' c4 'player'
MTB > info

COLUMN      NAME       COUNT
C1          ruth         15
C2          maris        10
C3          homeruns     25
C4          player       25

CONSTANTS USED: NONE

MTB > print c1-c4

   ROW    ruth    maris    homeruns    player

     1      54        8          54         1
     2      59       13          59         1
     3      35       14          35         1
     4      41       16          41         1
     5      46       23          46         1
     6      25       26          25         1
     7      47       28          47         1
     8      60       33          60         1
     9      54       39          54         1
    10      46       61          46         1
    11      49                   49         1
    12      46                   46         1
    13      41                   41         1
    14      34                   34         1
    15      22                   22         1
    16                            8         2
    17                           13         2
    18                           14         2
    19                           16         2
    20                           23         2
    21                           26         2
    22                           28         2
    23                           33         2
    24                           39         2
    25                           61         2

MTB > dotp c3;
SUBC> by c4.
```

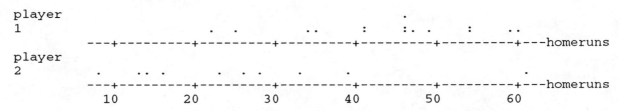

The **HISTogram** command has the same subcommands (**INCRement**, **STARt**, **BY**, and **SAME**) as the **DOTPlot** command, so two or more histograms using the same set of axes can be obtained in the same ways as described above. The subcommands **SAME** and **INCRement** are not available with the **STEM-and-leaf** command. Therefore, to obtain stem-and-leaf displays using the same axes, the subcommand **BY** must be used with the data in one column and codes in a second column.

The **TSPLot** Command

When data are collected over time, it is a good idea to plot the observations in the order they were collected. The **TSPLot** command is used to produce time series plots. **TSPLot** (the TS is for time series) plots the column of data (vertical axis) versus the integers 1, 2, 3, . . . (horizontal axis). The format for the command is listed below:

```
TSPLot  [period =  K] time series data in C
```

In the following example, we have stored the high temperature for Austin, Texas, for every day in May of 1991 in C1. The temperatures were recorded in Celsius and are printed and plotted below in a time series plot.

```
MTB > info

COLUMN      NAME         COUNT
C1                        31

CONSTANTS USED: NONE

MTB > print c1

C1
30     26     28     28     24     24     27     22     29     29     31     31
29     28     30     29     27     32     28     31     30     31     31     33
32     34     33     33     32     33     33
```

```
MTB > tsplot c1
```

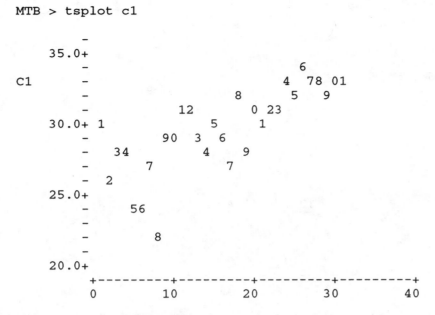

So that the observations can be followed through time, the first observation is coded "1," the second "2," and so on up to the tenth observation, which is labeled "0." The numbers repeat after the tenth observation. The time series plot above illustrates that the high temperatures had an upward trend in May.

The monthly sales figures (in $1000s) for an athletic shoe store are presented below for the years 1988, 1989, and 1990.

```
MTB > name c1 'sales'
MTB > print 'sales'

sales
204    188    235    227    234    264    302    293    259    229
203    229    242    233    267    269    270    315    364    347
312    274    237    278    284    277    317    313    318    374
413    405    355    306    271    306
```

Plotting these data as a time series will allow us to observe any trend or seasonal effects in the data. To identify the months, a period (K) may be specified in the **TSPLot** command. K may be any integer from 1 to 36. If a period is specified, the first observation is plotted with 1, the second with 2, until the end of the first period. Then the next observation is plotted with 1, then 2, etc. If the period is longer than 9, then 0 is used for 10, A for 11, . . . , Z for 36.

Coding the data to correspond to the months of the year, with a period of 12 (K = 12), will facilitate the identification of seasonal effects. If data are collected on a quarterly basis, then the appropriate period is 4. Similarly, if the data are collected on an hourly basis, the appropriate period is 24. Below we illustrate the use of a specified period with the monthly sales data.

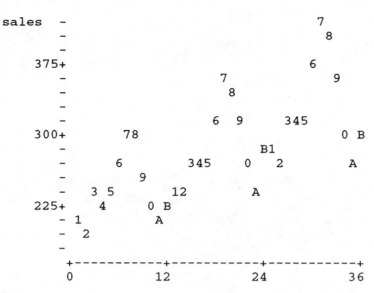

```
MTB > tsplot 12 'sales'

  sales  -                                               7
         -                                                 8
         -
    375+                                          6
         -                         7                          9
         -                           8
         -
         -                       6   9       345
    300+            78                                  0  B
         -                              B1
         -         6             345    0     2              A
         -            9
         -        3  5         12             A
    225+        4          0  B
         -   1                 A
         -   2
         -
         +-----------+-----------+-----------+
         0          12          24          36
```

Since the interval is specified as 12, the eleventh observation in each year is coded "A," and the twelfth observation with "B," making this time series plot easier to read. Since the numbers correspond to the months of the year, it is easy to see that the peaks in athletic shoe sales occur in the month of July (7 = July). The low points occur in November (A = November).

It is important that the observations in time series data occur at regular time intervals when using the **TSPLot** command. Often in time series data, some observations will be missing. To act as a placeholder for the missing time period, Minitab allows the entry of these missing observations through the use of the asterisk (*). The asterisk may be entered as an observation when using either the **READ** or the **SET** command or using the **INSErt** command.

Describing Distributions

Numerical measures are often used to describe distributions. The **DESCribe** command summarizes several different measures of both the center and variability of a distribution. The **DESCribe** command prints the statistics N, NMISS, MEAN, MEDIAN, TRMEAN, STDEV, SEMEAN, MAX, MIN, Q3, Q1 for each column specified. The format for the **DESCribe** command is

```
DESCribe the data in C,...,C
```

Below we illustrate the use of the **DESCribe** command using the home run data for Babe Ruth and Roger Maris.

```
MTB > describe c1 c2
```

	N	MEAN	MEDIAN	TRMEAN	STDEV	SEMEAN
ruth	15	43.93	46.00	44.38	11.25	2.90
maris	10	26.10	24.50	24.00	15.61	4.94

	MIN	MAX	Q1	Q3
ruth	22.00	60.00	35.00	54.00
maris	8.00	61.00	13.75	34.50

N is the number of actual values in the column (missing values are not counted). NMISS is the number of missing values. MEAN is the average of the values. To find the MEDIAN, the data first must be ordered. If N is odd, the MEDIAN is the value in the middle. If N is even, the median is the average of the two middle values. The TRMEAN, or trimmed mean, removes the smallest 5% and the largest 5% of the observations (rounded to the nearest integer) and averages the rest. STDEV is the standard deviation computed as

$$STDEV_x = \sqrt{\frac{\sum (x - \bar{x})}{N - 1}}$$

SEMEAN is the standard error of the mean. It is calculated as $STDEV/\sqrt{N}$. MAX is the maximum of the observations; MIN is the minimum of the observations.

Q3 is the third quartile and Q1 is the first quartile. Minitab doesn't use exactly the same algorithm to calculate quartiles as *I.P.S.*, so minor differences in results will sometimes occur. Use the **HELP** command to find out how the **DESCribe** command calculates the quartiles.

The commands **N**, **NMISs**, **MEAN**, **MEDIan**, **STDev**, **MINimum**, and **MAXimum** can also be used to obtain these measures for a column of data. In each command, the answer is printed if it is not stored. The command formats are

```
COUNt the number of values in C [put into K]
N (number of nonmissing values) for C [put into K]
NMISs the number of missing values in C [put into K]
MEAN of values in C [put mean into K]
MEDIan of the values in C [put into K]
STDev of C [put into K]
MINimum of the values in C [put into K]
MAXimum of the values in C [put into K]
```

For example, the command

```
MTB > MEAN C1 put into K1
```

will put the value 43.93 into the constant K1. The same result may also be obtained using the **LET** command as follows:

```
MTB > LET K1 = MEAN(C1)
```

Minitab will allow either command format for any of the above statistical operators.

The statistics we have just described are also available for rows. These commands compute summaries across rows rather than down columns. The answers are always stored in a column. The command formats are

```
RCOUnt E,...,E put the count of each row into C

RN E,...,E put number of nonmissing in each row into C

RNMIss E,...,E put number of missing in each row into C

RMEAn E,...,E put mean of each row into C

RMEDian E,...,E put median of each row into C

RSTDev E,...,E put standard deviation of each row into C

RMAXimum E,...,E put maximum of each row into C

RMINimum E,...,E put minimum of each row into C
```

For the commands **RMEAn, RMEDian, RSTDev, RMAXimum,** and **RMINimum,** as well as for **MEAN, MEDian, STDev, MAXimum,** and **MINimum,** missing observations are omitted from the calculations.

The **BOXPlot** Command

The five-number summary consisting of the median, quartiles, and minimum and maximum values provides a quick overall description of a distribution. Boxplots based on the five-number summary display the main features of a column of data. Boxplots can be obtained with the following format.

```
BOXPlot for data in C
```

A boxplot graphically displays the main features of data from a single variable. The middle half of each variable is represented by a box and the median is marked with a "+." Minitab calculates the middle half of the data using hinges. These are similar to, but not exactly the same as, quartiles. Although the boxplots computed by Minitab are slightly different from those described in *I.P.S.*, they are still useful for comparing several distributions. To do this, the subcommand **BY** is often used with the **BOXPlot** command. Below we illustrate the use of the boxplot displays to examine the home run distributions of Babe Ruth and Roger Maris.

```
MTB > boxp c3;
SUBC> by c4.

player
```

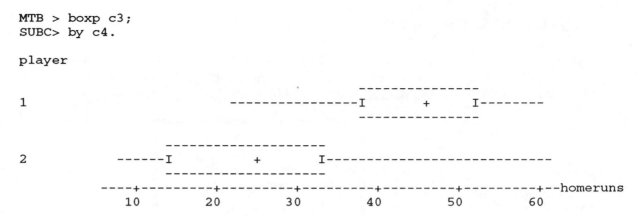

Possible outliers are marked on boxplots with an asterisk (*). Probable outliers are marked on the boxplot with a "0." To illustrate, we consider Newcomb's light measurement data, listed below and included in Table 1.1 (page 3) of *I.P.S.* These data has been stored in NEWCOMB.MTW.

```
MTB > retr 'NEWCOMB.MTW'
 WORKSHEET SAVED  6/26/1992

Worksheet retrieved from file: NEWCOMB.MTW

MTB > print c1

speed
    28    26    33    24    34   -44    27    16    40    -2    29
    22    24    21    25    30    23    29    31    19    24    20
    36    32    36    28    25    21    28    29    37    25    28
    26    30    32    36    26    30    22    36    23    27    27
    28    27    31    27    26    33    26    32    32    24    39
    28    24    25    32    25    29    27    28    29    16    23

MTB > boxp c1
```

While no possible outliers are shown in the above boxplot, the observations −2 and −44 are probable outliers and are marked with zeroes.

The criteria for possible and probable outliers cannot guarantee that all extreme values will be identified. For example, Roger Maris's exceptional performance of 61 homers in 1961 is not identified as an outlier in the boxplot above.

The LET Command

Recall that in the introductory chapter, the **LET** command was used to correct individual data point entries. In addition to that function, the **LET** command can be used to do arithmetic using the following operations.

+	Addition
−	Subtraction
*	Multiplication
/	Division
**	Exponentiation

Additional Minitab functions such as **MEAN, STDev, ROUNd, SQRT, LOGTen, LOGE, EXPOnentiate, N, MAX,** and **MIN** can also be used as part of the expression on the righthand side of the **LET** command.

For example, linear transformations of the form $x^* = a + bx$ can be obtained using the **LET** command. In the following example, we have stored the high temperature for Austin, Texas, for every day in May of 1991 in column C1. The temperatures were recorded in Celsius. A linear transformation is required to change the data to degrees Fahrenheit: $^\circ F = 32 + 9/5(^\circ C)$.

```
MTB > print c1

C1
30      26      28      28      24      24      27      22      29      29      31      31
29      28      30      29      27      32      28      31      30      31      31      33
32      34      33      33      32      33      33

MTB > let c2 = 32 + 9/5 * c1
MTB > print c2

C2
86.0    78.8    82.4    82.4    75.2    75.2    80.6    71.6    84.2    84.2
87.8    87.8    84.2    82.4    86.0    84.2    80.6    89.6    82.4    87.8
86.0    87.8    87.8    91.4    89.6    93.2    91.4    91.4    89.6    91.4
91.4
MTB > mean c1
   MEAN      =       29.613
MTB > mean c2
   MEAN      =       85.303
```

Note that the mean is also transformed by multiplying by 9/5 and adding 32. That is, $85.303 = 32 + 9/5(29.613)$.

The **MEAN** command can only be used for one column at a time, since it has the following format.

```
      MEAN of the values in C [put mean into K]
```

If a second column is specified, then Minitab will put the result (the mean of the first column) into the second specified column. This is illustrated in the example given below.

```
      MTB > mean c1 c2
         MEAN     =      29.613
      MTB > print c1 c2

        ROW     C1          C2

          1     30       29.613
          2     26
          3     28
          4     28
                 .
                 .
                 .
                 .
         28     33
         29     32
         30     33
         31     33
```

Similarly, the commands **STDev, ROUNd, SQRT, LOGTen, LOGE, EXPOnentiate, MAXimum,** and **MINimum** can be used for only one column at a time.

Normal Distributions

Minitab can be used to perform normal distribution calculations. If data in a column are normally distributed, then the **LET** command can be used to obtain the standardized values, that is, those with mean equal to 0 and standard deviation equal to 1. In C1, we have stored the exam scores for a class of 40 students. Using the **MEAN** and **STDev** commands, we can find the mean and standard deviation for the exam scores and store them as K1 and K2. The stored values can be used with the **LET** command, and the standardized values, $z^* = (x - \bar{x})/s$, can be stored in C2 as illustrated below.

```
      MTB > print c1

      C1
         58    98    57    70    60    62    74    75    81    99    49
         75    71    86    73    90    82    74    63    61    55    80
         52   100    75    58    63    66    68    55   100    91   100
         66    84    36    90    75    89    78    84    84    87    83
         79    65    43    65    75    78

      MTB > mean c1 k1
         MEAN     =      73.660
      MTB > std c1 k2
         ST.DEV. =      15.218
      MTB > let c2 = (c1-k1)/k2
```

```
MTB > print c2

C2
-1.02907    1.59946   -1.09478   -0.24051   -0.89764   -0.76622    0.02234
 0.08806    0.48234    1.66517   -1.62049    0.08806   -0.17480    0.81090
-0.04337    1.07376    0.54805    0.02234   -0.70050   -0.83193   -1.22621
 0.41662   -1.42335    1.73089    0.08806   -1.02907   -0.70050   -0.50336
-0.37194   -1.22621    1.79660    1.13947    1.73089   -0.50336    0.67948
-2.47476    1.07376    0.08806    1.00804    0.28520    0.67948    0.67948
 0.87662    0.61376    0.35091   -0.56908   -2.01477   -0.56908    0.08806
 0.28520
```

The standardized test scores will tell how far above or below the mean an individual scored. The measure is in units of standard deviations. For example, the first score, 58, is just slightly more than 1 standard deviation ($z = -1.02907$) below the mean. The second score, 98, is nearly 1.6 standard deviations ($z = 1.59946$) above the mean.

The CDF Command

The **CDF** command calculates the cummulative distribution function for a variety of distributions. That is, for any distribution, it gives the relative frequency of observations that are less than or equal to the given value. The command format is

```
CDF for values in E [store results in E]
```

If a subcommand is not used with the **CDF** command, a standard normal with $\mu = 0$ and $\sigma = 1$ is assumed. That is, if X has the $N(\mu,\sigma)$ distribution, then the standardized variable $Z = (X - \mu)/\sigma$ has the standard normal distribution $N(0, 1)$. Relative frequencies for the event $Z < z$ can be calculated using the CDF command instead of Table A in *I.P.S.* In the following example, the relative frequencies for values in C2 are obtained (using $\bar{x}$ for μ and s for σ) and stored in C3.

```
MTB > cdf c2 c3
MTB > name c1 'x'
MTB > name c2 'z'
MTB > name c3 'freq'
MTB > print c1-c3

ROW      x         z        freq

  1     58   -1.02907    0.151723
  2     98    1.59946    0.945141
  3     57   -1.09478    0.136806
       .
       .
       .
 39     75    0.08806    0.535084
 40     78    0.28520    0.612253
```

The example illustrates that the score of 58 ($z = -1.02907$) has approximately 15% of the scores below it (freq = 0.151723) and the score of 98 ($z = 1.59946$) has approximately 95% of the scores below it (freq = 0.945141).

The NSCOres and PLOT Commands

Normal quantile plots (or normal probability plots) are useful for assessing normality. The plots are constructed in Minitab using the **NSCOres** and **PLOT** commands. The **NSCOres** command is used to calculate normal scores and has the following format:

```
NSCOres of C, put into C
```

The **NSCOres** command calculates the normal scores for a column that is assumed to have a perfect normal distribution. For example, the normal score for the median value in a column of data will be 0. By plotting data versus the normal scores (obtained with the **NSCOres** command) it is possible to see how different actual data are from a perfect normal distribution. The **PLOT** command has the following format:

```
PLOT C vs C
```

Deviations of the points on such a plot from a straight line show deviations of the data from normality. The following example illustrates the use of the **NSCOres** and **PLOT** commands to generate a normal plot using Minitab.

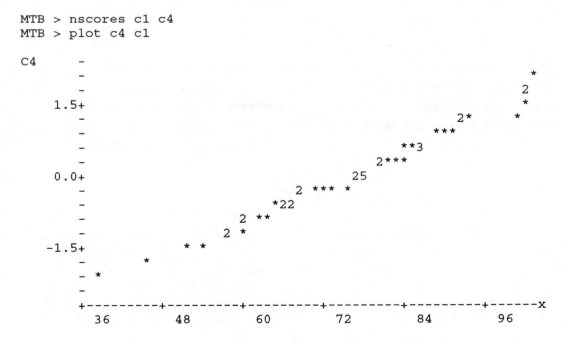

The first column specified with the **PLOT** command is the vertical axis; the second is horizontal. Each point is plotted with the symbol *. If more than one point falls on a plotting position, a count is given. If the count is over 9, a + is used. The normal plot generated illustrates that the test scores in C1 are approximately normal with the upper tail less extreme than expected.

The RANDom Command

The **RANDom** command generates random observations, from the distribution specified in the subcommand, into each of the columns specified. The command format is

```
RANDom K observations into each of C,...,C
```

If you do not use a subcommand, Minitab generates data from a normal distribution with $\mu = 0$ and $\sigma = 1$. If you want to specify a normal distribution with another mean and variance, the following subcommand format can be used.

```
NORMal [mu = K [sigma = K]]
```

Suppose you want 50 samples, each of size 3, from a normal distribution with $\mu = 20$ and $\sigma = 5$. There are two ways you can use the **RANDom** command.

```
MTB > random 50 c1-c3;
SUBC> normal 20 5.
```

puts each sample of size 3 into each of 50 rows. In this case, commands like **MEAN** and **STDev** can be used to calculate summary statistics.

```
MTB > random 3 c1-c50;
SUBC> normal 20 5.
```

puts each sample of size 3 into each of 50 columns. In this case, commands like **RMEAn** and **RSTDev** can be used to calculate and store summary statistics into a column. If a normal quantile plot is constructed (using **NSCOres** and **PLOT** commands) to assess the normality of data obtained using the **RANDom** command, a perfect straight line will not usually be obtained; however, the data will be *approximately* normal.

EXERCISES

1.11 A quality engineer in an automobile engine plant measures a critical dimension on each of a sample of crankshafts at regular intervals. The dimension is supposed to be 224 millimeters (mm), but some variation will occur in production. The latest measurements are given below and stored in CRANK.MTW.

224.120	224.001	224.017	223.982	223.989	223.961
223.960	224.089	223.987	223.976	223.902	223.980
224.098	224.057	223.913	223.999		

(a)   The engineer *codes* these measurements to make them easier to work with. The coded value is the number of thousandths of a millimeter above 223 mm. (For example, 224.120 mm is coded as 1120.) Use the **LET** command to find the coded value for each of the measurements in the sample. (Hint: You may also want to use the **ROUNd** command to ensure that you obtain whole numbers.) Use the **SAVE** command to save the data set with the original and coded values.

(b)   Make a **STEM-and-leaf** display for the data after you have coded the original measurements. Make a stemplot of the original data. Describe and compare the shape of the two distributions.

(c)   Make a **HISTogram** of the original and coded data. Do you prefer the stemplots or the histograms? Explain your answer.

1.17   The Survey of Study Habits and Attitudes (SSHA) is a psychological test that evaluates college students' motivation, study habits, and attitudes toward school. A selective private college gives the SSHA to a sample of its incoming freshmen. The data are given in SSHA.MTW. The scores for a sample of 18 women are

| 154 | 109 | 137 | 115 | 152 | 140 | 154 | 178 | 101 |
| 103 | 126 | 126 | 137 | 165 | 165 | 129 | 200 | 148 |

(a)   Make a **STEM-and-leaf** display of these data. The overall shape of the distribution is indistinct, as often happens when only a few observations are available. Are there any outliers?

(b)   Use the **DESCribe** command to find the mean score and the median score for this group. Explain the relationship between these two measures in terms of the main features of the distribution of scores.

(c)   The scores for a sample of 20 men are

| 108 | 140 | 114 | 91 | 180 | 115 | 126 | 92 | 169 | 146 |
| 109 | 132 | 75 | 88 | 113 | 151 | 70 | 115 | 187 | 104 |

(d)   Make **STEM-and-leaf** displays of the men's and women's scores using the same scales. What is the most noticeable contrast between the two distributions?

(e)   Make **BOXPlots** of the distributions using the same scales. (Hint: Use the **STACk** command with the **SUBScripts** subcommand.) Are any outliers or suspected outliers identified?

1.18   Here are data on the percent of residents 65 years of age and over in each of the 50 states. The data are also given in ELDERLY.MTW.

AL	12.5	HI	10.4	MA	13.7	NM	10.3	SD	14.0
AK	3.8	ID	11.7	MI	11.7	NY	13.0	TN	12.5
AZ	12.8	IL	12.2	MN	12.5	NC	11.9	TX	9.9
AR	14.6	IN	12.2	MS	12.3	ND	13.5	UT	8.4
CA	10.6	IA	14.9	MO	13.8	OH	12.6	VT	11.8
CO	9.5	KS	13.5	MT	12.8	OK	13.0	VA	10.6
CT	13.4	KY	12.4	NE	13.8	OR	13.8	WA	11.8
DE	11.6	LA	10.9	NV	10.7	PA	14.9	WV	14.3
FL	17.8	ME	13.4	NH	11.3	RI	14.7	WI	13.2
GA	10.0	MD	10.8	NJ	13.1	SC	10.9	WY	9.4

(a)   Make a stemplot of these data using percent as stems and tenths of a percent as leaves. Then make a second stemplot splitting each stem in two (using the subcommand **INCRement**. Which display do you prefer?

(b)   Describe the shape of the distribution. Is is roughly symmetric or distinctly skewed? Where is the center of the distribution? Are there clear outliers?

(c)   Give a brief numerical summary of the distribution of percent of residents over 65 by state. Explain your choice of numerical measures.

1.19   Thomas the cat is helping researchers study the fleas that cause discomfort to him and his fellow cats. One part of the research concerns the egg production of the flea *Ctenocephalides felis*. The researchers deposit 25 female and 10 male fleas in Thomas's fur and count the number of flea eggs produced each day. The number of eggs produced by the fleas in 27 consecutive days is stored in FLEA.MTW and is given below. (Data provided by Sayed Gaafar and Michael Dryden, Purdue University School of Veterinary Medicine.)

436	495	575	444	754	915	945	655	782	704
590	411	547	584	550	487	585	549	475	435
523	390	425	415	450	395	405			

(a)   Present the distribution in a **STEM-and-leaf** display. Describe the general shape and the center of the distribution. Are there any unusual values?

(b)   Based on the shape of the distribution and the presence or absence of outliers, would you prefer the median and quartiles or the mean and standard deviation as a helpful numerical summary? Use Minitab to compute the summary that you have chosen.

1.20   Climatologists interested in flooding gather statistics on the daily rainfall in various cities. The following data set gives the *maximum* daily rainfall (in inches) for each of the years 1941 to 1970 in South Bend, Indiana. The data are also given in RAIN.MTW. (Successive years follow each other across the rows in the table.)

1.88	2.23	2.58	2.07	2.94	2.29	3.14	2.15	1.95	2.51
2.86	1.48	1.12	2.76	3.10	2.05	2.23	1.70	1.57	2.81
1.24	3.29	1.87	1.50	2.99	3.48	2.12	4.69	2.29	2.12

(a) Make a **STEM-and-leaf** display for these data. Describe the general shape of the distribution and any prominent deviations from the overall pattern.

(b) Compute the five-number summary for these data using the **DESCribe** command.

(c) Make a **BOXPlot** of the data. Are there any outliers or suspected outliers identified?

(d) The *trimmed* mean is a measure of center that is more resistant than the mean but uses more of the available information than the median. To compute the 5% trimmed mean, discard the highest 5% and the lowest 5% of the observations and compute the mean of the remaining 90%. Trimming eliminates the effect of a small number of outliers. The **DESCribe** command computes the 5% trimmed mean. Compare the values of these measures with the median and the ordinary untrimmed mean.

(e) Use the **NSCOres** and **PLOT** commands to produce a normal quantile plot of the maximum rainfall data. Are there any clear deviations from normality?

1.22 The *Old Farmer's Almanac* gives the growing season for major U.S. cities as reported by the National Climatic Center. The growing season is defined as the average number of days between the last frost in the spring and the first frost in the fall. The following values are stored in GROWING.MTW.

279	244	318	262	335	321	165	180	201	252
145	192	217	179	182	210	271	302	169	192
156	181	156	125	166	248	198	220	134	189
141	142	211	196	169	237	136	203	184	224
178	279	201	173	252	149	229	300	217	203
148	220	175	188	160	176	128			

(a) Make a **STEM-and-leaf** display for these data. Describe the general shape of the distribution. Are there any unusual values?

(b) Make a **BOXPlot** of the distribution of the growing season data. Are there any outliers or suspected outliers identified?

1.23 There are many ways to measure the reading ability of children. Research designed to improve reading performance requires good measures of the outcome. One frequently used test is the DRP, or Degree of Reading Power. In a research study on third grade students, the DRP was administered to 44 students. Their scores are given below and stored in DRP.MTW. (Data provided by Maribeth Cassidy Schmitt, from her Ph.D dissertation, *The effects of an elaborated directed reading activity on the metacomprehension skills of third graders*, Purdue University, 1987.)

40	26	39	14	42	18	25	43	46	27	19
47	19	26	35	34	15	44	40	38	31	46
52	25	35	35	33	29	34	41	49	28	52
47	35	48	22	33	41	51	27	14	54	45

(a)   Make a **STEM-and-leaf** display of these data. Then make a **HISTogram**. Which display do you prefer, and why? Describe the main features of the distribution.

(b)   Use the **NSCOres** and **PLOT** commands to produce a normal quantile plot of the DRP reading scores. Are the mean and standard deviation adequate measures of center and spread for these data? If so, calculate the mean and standard deviation.

1.25   In 1798 the English scientist Henry Cavendish measured the density of the earth by careful work with a torsion balance. The variable recorded was the density of the earth as a multiple of the density of water. Below and in EARTH.MTW are Cavendish's 29 measurements. (Cavendish's data are reported by S. M. Stigler "Do robust estimators work with real data?" *Annals of Statistics*, 5(177), pp. 1055-1078.

5.50	5.61	4.88	5.07	5.26	5.55	5.36	5.29	5.58	5.65
5.57	5.53	5.62	5.29	5.44	5.34	5.79	5.10	5.27	5.39
5.42	5.47	5.63	5.34	5.46	5.30	5.75	5.68	5.85	

(a)   Present these measurements by a **STEM-and-leaf** display and a **HISTogram**. Which display do you prefer? Then briefly discuss the main features of the distribution. In particular, what is your estimate of the density of the earth based on these measurements?

(b)   Compute the mean and standard deviation. Based on the general shape of this distribution, would you be willing to report the mean and standard deviation as helpful descriptive measures? If so, the mean would be used to estimate the actual density of the earth.

(c)   Make a normal quantile plot for Cavendish's measurements. Are the data approximately normal? If not, describe any clear deviations from normality.

1.28   Plant scientists have developed varieties of corn that have increased amounts of the essential amino acid lysine. In a test of the protein quality of this corn, an experimental group of 20 one-day-old male chicks was fed a ration containing the new corn. A control group of another 20 chicks was fed a ration that was identical except that it contained normal corn. Here and in CORN.MTW are the weight gains (in grams) after 21 days. (Based on G. L. Cromwell et al., "A comparison of the nutritive value of *opaque-2, floury-2* and normal corn for the chick," *Poultry Science*, 47 (1968), pp. 840–847.)

Control				Experimental			
380	321	366	356	361	447	401	375
283	349	402	462	434	403	393	426
356	410	329	399	406	318	467	407
350	384	316	272	427	420	477	392
345	455	360	431	430	339	410	326

(a)   Make **DOTPlots** of these data using the same scale. Does it appear that the chicks fed high-lysine corn grew faster? Are there any outliers or other problems?

(b)   Make **BOXPlots** on the same scales to compare the distributions. Write a short statement about the observed differences, backing your claims by citing appropriate numbers.

(c)   Make a normal quantile plot for each group. Are the distributions approximately normal?

(d)   Summarize the distributions by computing the mean and standard deviation for each group. Did the high-lysine chicks gain more weight? Is the variability in weight gains substantially different in the two groups?

1.32   The years around 1970 brought unrest to many U.S. cities. Here are data on the number of civil disturbances in each 3-month period during the years 1968 to 1972. The data are also given in RIOTS.MTW.

Period		Count	Period		Count
1968,	Jan.-Mar.	6	1970,	July-Sept.	20
	Apr.-June	46		Oct.-Dec.	6
	July-Sept.	25	1971,	Jan.-Mar.	12
	Oct.-Dec.	3		Apr.-June	21
1969,	Jan.-Mar.	5		July-Sept.	5
	Apr.-June	27		Oct.-Dec.	1
	July-Sept.	19	1972,	Jan.-Mar.	3
	Oct.-Dec.	6		Apr.-June	8
1970,	Jan.-Mar.	26		July-Sept.	5
	Apr.-June	24		Oct.-Dec.	5

(a)   Use the **TSPLot** command with the period specified to make a time plot of these counts. Use a pencil to connect the points in your plot by straight line segments to make the pattern clearer.

(b)   Describe the trend and seasonal variation in this time series. Can you suggest an explanation for the seasonal variation in civil disorders?

1.33   We often look at time series data to see the effect of a social change or new policy. Below and in DEATHS.MTW are data on motor vehicle deaths in the United States. Because the *number* of deaths will tend to rise as motorists drive more miles, we look instead at the *rate* of deaths, which is the number of deaths per 100 million miles driven.

Year	Rate	Year	Rate
1960	5.1	1974	3.5
1962	5.1	1976	3.3
1964	5.4	1978	3.3
1966	5.5	1980	3.3
1968	5.2	1982	2.8
1970	4.7	1984	2.6
1972	4.3	1986	2.5
		1988	2.4

(a)   Make a **TSPLot** of these death rates. Describe the overall pattern of the data.

(b)   In 1974 the national speed limit was lowered to 55 miles per hour in an attempt to conserve gasoline after the 1973 Mideast war. In the mid-1980s most states raised speed limits on interstate highways to 65 miles per hour. Some said that the lower speed limit saved lives. Is the effect of lower speed limits between 1974 and the mid-1980s visible in your plot?

1.34   Babe Ruth was a pitcher for the Boston Red Sox in the years 1914 to 1917. In 1918 and 1919 he played some games as a pitcher and some as an outfielder. From 1920 to 1934 Ruth was an outfielder for the New York Yankees. He ended his career in 1935 with the Boston Braves. Here and in RUTH.MTW are the number of home runs Ruth hit in each year.

1914	1915	1916	1917	1918	1919	1920	1921	1922	1923	1924
0	4	3	2	11	29	54	59	35	41	46

1925	1926	1927	1928	1929	1930	1931	1932	1933	1934	1935
25	47	60	54	46	49	46	41	34	22	6

Earlier we examined the distribution of Ruth's home run totals during his Yankee years. Now make a **TSPLot** and describe its main features.

1.35   Here are the numbers of international airline passengers (in thousands) for each month of the years 1954 to 1956. The data are also stored in AIRLINE.MTW. Use the **TSPLot** command with the period specified to plot this time series. Identify the major patterns present (trend, cycles, seasonal variation). Suggest an explanation for the patterns that you see. (Part of a larger data set given by G. E. P. Box and G. M. Jenkins, *Time Series Analysis*, Holden-Day, Oakland, Calif., 1976, p. 531.)

Month	1954	1955	1956
JAN	204	242	284
FEB	188	233	277
MAR	235	267	317
APR	227	269	313
MAY	234	270	318
JUN	264	315	374
JUL	302	364	413
AUG	293	347	405
SEP	259	312	355
OCT	229	274	306
NOV	203	237	271
DEC	229	278	306

1.43   In Exercise 1.11, you were asked to code the crankshaft measurements.

   (a)   Use the **RETRieve** command to restore CRANK.MTW data set.

   (b)   Compute the mean and median of these measurements. Explain the relationship between the two measures of center in terms of the symmetry or skewness of the distribution. Find the mean and median for the coded data.

   (c)   Compute the standard deviation of the crankshaft measurements before and after coding. If you used the **DESCribe** command to do part (b)., just find the correct values. Based on the general shape of this distribution, would you be willing to report the mean and standard deviation as helpful descriptive measures?

1.66   CALORIES.MTW and the data below give the calorie content of a number of brands of beef, meat, and poultry hot dogs. We would like to compare the distribution of calories in the three types of hot dogs.

beef	186	181	176	149	184	190	158	139	175	148
	152	111	141	153	190	157	131	149	135	132
meat	173	191	182	190	172	147	146	139	175	136
	179	153	107	195	135	140	138			
poultry	129	132	102	106	94	102	87	99	107	113
	135	142	86	143	152	146	144			

   (a)   Use the **DESCribe** command to summarize the distributions of calories for the three types of hotdogs.

   (b)   Make **BOXPlots** using the same scales for the three distributions of sodium content. Comment on any differences between the distributions.

   (c)   Use the **NSCOres** and **PLOT** commands to make normal quantile plots for the calorie content of each of the three types of hot dogs. Then briefly compare the three distributions on the basis of their normal quantile plots.

1.94   The distribution of a critical dimension on auto engine crankshafts is approximately normal with $\mu = 224$ mm and $\sigma = 0.03$ mm. Crankshafts with dimensions between 223.92 mm and 224.08 mm are acceptable.

(a)   Use the **CDF** command to determine what percent of all crankshafts produced should be acceptable.

(b)   The **CODE** command can be used to identify the acceptable crankshafts from the sample of 16 saved in CRANK.MTW. To learn more about the **CODE** command, use the **HELP** command. The following commands will create and print C3 in which acceptable crankshaft measurements are coded 1 and unacceptable measurements are coded 0.

```
MTB > code (223.92:224.08) 1 (220:223.92) 0 (224.08:230) 0 c1 c3
MTB > print c1 c3
```

Use the **MEAN** command to determine the percent of the 16 crankshafts that are acceptable.

(c)   Use the **RANDom** command with the **NORMal** subcommand to simulate 100 crankshaft measurements with a normal distribution with mean 224 and standard deviation 0.03. Use the **CODE** and **MEAN** commands to determine the percent of the 100 simulated measurements that are acceptable.

(d)   Use the **NSCOres** and **PLOT** commands to make a normal quantile plot of the crankshaft measurements. Are the data approximately normal? If not, how do they depart from normality?

1.108   The following table and BASEBALL.MTW give the 1990 baseball income (in thousands of dollars) for the members of the Chicago Cubs. (Data from *The New York Times*, April 10, 1991.)

Dawson	3300	Assenmacher	1000	Dascenzo	165
Sandberg	2650	Bielecki	810	Boskie	130
Jackson	2625	Salizar	575	Villaneuva	120
Maddux	2400	Lancaster	550	Vizcaino	114
Sutcliffe	2275	Berryhill	230	McElroy	111
Bell	2100	Girardi	225	Scott	100
Dunston	2100	Smith	225	Pappas	100
Smith	1900	Harkey	220	Slocumb	100
Grace	1200	Walton	210	Walker	100

(a)   Examine this distribution, present it graphically and numerically in the way you think appropriate, and describe the notable features of the distribution.

(b)   Compute a new variable which is salary in excess of the minimum salary in thousands of dollars. That is, use the **LET** command to define SALNEW = SALARY − 100.

(c)   Compute the five-number summary, the IQR, the mean, and the standard deviation for the salaries as given and for the the new variable. For each numerical summary explain how the value for the new variable is related to the value for salary.

(d) Is the shape of the distribution changed by the transformation? Explain why or why not.

1.119 The following table and FOOTBALL.MTW give the weights in pounds of the players on a Big Ten football team as listed in the team's preseason publicity brochure. We will investigate the shape of this distribution.

160	165	202	245	150	235	241	195	181	256
200	265	168	233	215	185	185	185	263	214
230	260	190	185	294	180	179	295	175	157
218	208	145	205	210	171	276	220	180	222
175	170	157	195	260	186	225	188	260	192
214	266	265	188	196	228	270	163	183	160
260	178	260	155	210	200	276	290	165	220
210	200	185	195	196	260	165	175	224	235
225	228	215	225	229	214	193	162	294	280
183	185	263	276	290	218	184	190	180	225
220	250	253	220	155	160	176	200	230	218
158	215	225	184	195	282	252	218	235	182
180	180	180	224	214	210	255	270	200	234
175									

(a) Make either a **STEM-and-leaf** display or a **HISTogram**, and explain your choice of graphical display. Also make a normal quantile plot.

(b) Describe the main features of the distribution. Is it symmetric? Approximately normal? Does it appear that there are groups of players with different weight distributions, such as linemen and defensive backs? Are there any outliers?

(c) Give a brief numerical summary chosen in the light of your findings in (b).

(d) For publication you must restate your summary in kilograms rather than pounds; do this. (One kilogram equals 2.2 pounds, so 160 pounds is 72.73 kg.)

(e) There is a special kind of granularity in this data set; describe it. (Hint: Look at the last digit.)

1.120 The data below are the survival times of 72 guinea pigs after they were injected with tubercle bacilli in a medical experiment. These data are stored in PIGS.MTW. (Data from T. Bjerkedal, "Acquisition of resistance in guinea pigs infected with different doses of virulent tubercle bacilli," *American Journal of Hygiene*, 72 (1960), pp. 130–148.)

43	45	53	56	56	57	58	66	67
73	74	79	80	80	81	81	81	82
83	83	84	88	89	91	91	92	92
97	99	99	100	100	101	102	102	102
103	104	107	108	109	113	114	118	121
123	126	128	137	138	139	144	145	147
156	162	174	178	179	184	191	198	211
214	243	249	329	380	403	511	522	598

Give a brief graphical and numerical description of this distribution, using the methods you think are most appropriate. Briefly describe the main features of the distribution.

1.121 With the following Minitab commands, produce 100 observations from the $N(20, 5)$ distribution and then compute several descriptive measures for these observations.

```
MTB > RANDOM 100 C1;
SUBC> NORMAL 20, 5.
MTB > DESCRIBE C1
```

(a)   Compute the mean, $\bar{x}$ and standard deviation, s of the 25 values you obtain. How close are $\bar{x}$ and s to $\mu = 20$ and $\sigma = 5$?

(b)   Repeat 20 times the process of generating 25 observations from the $N(20, 5)$ distribution and recording $\bar{x}$ and s. Make a stemplot of the 20 values of $\bar{x}$ and another stemplot of the 20 values of s. Briefly describe each of these distributions. Are they symmetric or skewed? Where are their centers? (The distributions of measures like $\bar{x}$ and s when repeated sets of observations are made from the same theoretical distribution will be very important in later chapters.)

1.123 The CHEESE.MTW data set described in the data appendix (page 791) of *I.P.S.* records measurements on 30 specimens of Australian cheddar cheese. Investigate the distributions of the variables H2S and LACTIC using graphical and numerical summaries of your choice. Write a short description of the notable features for each distribution.

1.124 The CSDATA.MTW data set described in the data appendix (page 792) of *I.P.S.* contains information on 224 computer science students. We are interested in comparing female students as a group to male students as a group. Gender was recorded as 1 for men and 2 for women.

(a)   Use **BOXPlots** on the same scales to compare men and women first on SAT mathematics score and then on college grade point average (GPA). Write a brief discussion of the male-female comparisons.

(b)   Make normal quantile plots of GPA and SAT math scores separately for men and women. Which of the four distributions are approximately normal?

Chapter 2
Looking at Data: Relationships

Commands to be covered in this chapter:

PLOT C vs C

LPLOt C vs C using labels as coded in C

CODE (K...K) to K ... (K...K) to K for C...C, store in C...C

MPLOt C vs C, and C vs C,..., and C vs C

REGRess C on 1 predictor C

LOGTen of E, put into E

CORRelate the data in C,...,C

TABLe the data classified by C,...,C

Scatterplots

Often we are interested in illustrating the relationships between two variables, such as the relationship between height and weight, between smoking and lung cancer, or between advertising expenditures and sales. For illustration, we will consider data from the sales of forty houses in Austin, Texas. Each row corresponds to a case: the sale of one house. The variables are selling price (in $1000s), area (in square feet), and the number of bedrooms. The data are provided below and in HOUSE.MTW.

```
MTB > info

COLUMN      NAME        COUNT
C1          price        40
C2          area         40
C3          beds         40

CONSTANTS USED: NONE

MTB > print c1-c3

ROW   price   area   beds

  1      72   1545      2
  2      78   1360      2
  3      92   1455      2
```

4	93	1373	3
5	94	1666	3
6	95	1634	3
7	95	1849	3
8	98	1507	3
9	99	1102	2
10	105	1621	3
11	107	1957	3
12	112	1523	4
13	115	1597	4
14	119	1740	2
15	121	2014	4
16	125	1716	4
17	129	1763	4
18	130	1554	4
19	130	2017	3
20	136	1803	4
21	136	1916	4
22	139	2210	3
23	140	2330	3
24	141	1930	4
25	146	2012	4
26	150	1842	3
27	150	2840	4
28	151	2032	4
29	162	2119	4
30	170	2532	3
31	172	2083	4
32	176	2920	3
33	183	3342	3
34	190	2295	4
35	197	3065	3
36	197	2311	4
37	199	2249	4
38	199	2953	3
39	205	3695	3
40	222	2681	4

The PLOT Command

If both variables are quantitative, the most useful display of their relationship is the scatterplot. Scatterplots can be produced using the **PLOT** command. Recall from Chapter 1 that the command format is

```
PLOT C vs C
```

The first column is the vertical axis; the second is the horizontal axis. Minitab represents single points with an asterisk (*). If more than one point falls on the same position on the graph, Minitab replaces the asterisk with a number, which represents the number of points at that location. If the number of points is greater than 9, Minitab uses a plus sign (+) to represent the points. Using the housing data from Austin, Texas, the command is illustrated below for a scatterplot of price versus area.

```
MTB > plot c1 c2

price  -
       -
       -                                                     *
 200+                                          **                    *  *
       -                                        *
       -                                                    *
       -                                *               *
 150+                            *   **                      *
       -                        * **           *   *
       -                *   **           *
       -                    *   *           *
       -                  *  *           *
 100+       *           *   *       *
       -           *  *       *
       -              *
       -                 *
       +---------+---------+---------+---------+---------+---------+------area
        1000      1500      2000      2500      3000      3500
```

To specify the scales on the *x* and *y* axes, the following subcommands are available: **XINCrement**, **XSTArt**, **YINCrement**, and **YSTArt**. **XSTArt** and **YSTArt** specify the first and optionally the last point plotted. **XINCrement** and **YINCrement** enable the user to specify the distance between the tick marks on the axes. The formats for these subcommands are

```
XINCrement  = K
XSTArt      = K
YINCrement  = K
YSTArt      = K
```

For example, to reduce the size of the above graph, the **XINCrement** could be doubled to 1000, and the **YINCrement** could be doubled to 100:

```
MTB > plot 'price' 'area';
SUBC> xstart 1000;
SUBC> xinc 1000;
SUBC> ystart 50;
SUBC> yinc 100.


       -
       -                        *
 200+                     *2        **        *
       -                   *    *    *    *
price  -               *  **         *
       -             * *22  **
       -            **2*  *
 100+      *    *22** *
       -            **

       -
       -
       +---------+---------+--------area
       1000      2000      3000
```

The LPLOt Command

We can add information about a third variable to a scatterplot by using different symbols for different points. The **LPLOt** command is used to plot data with labels. The format for plotting points with different labels is

```
LPLOT C vs C using labels as coded in C
```

The command plots the first two columns using plotting symbols that are specified by the numbers in the third column (these numbers must be integers). The plotting codes are

```
...-10 1 2 3 4 5 6 7 8 9 10 11 12 13 14 15 16 17 18 19 20 21 22 23 24 25 26 27...
...Y Z A B C D E F G H I J  K  L  M  N  O  P  Q  R  S  T  U  V  W  X  Y  Z  A...
```

If several points fall on the same spot, a count is given as in the **PLOT** command. If the count is over 9, a plus sign (+) is used. The command is illustrated below using the number of bedrooms (C3) as a categorical explanatory variable. From above, the plotting code for two-bedroom homes will be a "B," the plotting code for three-bedroom homes will be a "C," and the plotting code for four-bedroom homes will be a "D."

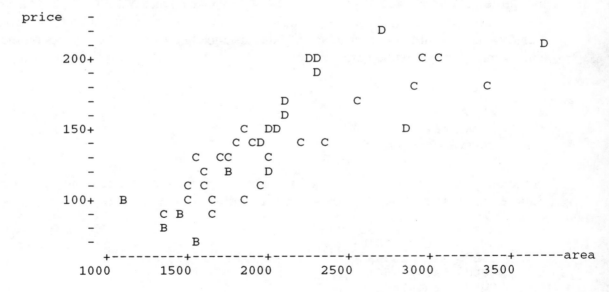

From the scatterplot, it seems that having a larger number of bedrooms tends to increase the price of a house.

The CODE Command

The **CODE** command copies columns, changing the indicated values according to the following format.

```
CODE (K...K) to K  ...  (K...K) to K for C...C, store in C...C
```

For example, the **CODE** command can be used to change a quantitative variable such as 'area' into a categorical variable. We will do this by assigning a code of 0 for homes with living area size between 1000 and 1500 square feet; a code of 1 for homes with areas between 1500 and 2000 square feet, and so on. The **CODE** command used below is too long to fit on one line, so an ampersand (&) is used to indicate that the command continues on the following line. A continuation prompt (CONT>) will follow the incomplete command ending with an ampersand.

```
MTB > code (1000:1500) 0 (1500:2000) 1 (2000:2500) 2 (2500:3000) &
CONT> 3 (3000:3500) 4 ( 3500:4000) 5 c2 c5
MTB > name c5 'size'
MTB > info

COLUMN     NAME        COUNT
C1         price         40
C2         area          40
C3         beds          40
C5         size          40

CONSTANTS USED: NONE
```

If two ranges in parentheses overlap, only the first one is used. If a home has area of exactly 1500 square feet, it will be coded as 0. Parentheses must always be used with the **CODE** command.

Below we use the coded values to create a median trace for the scatterplot of price versus area. The **DESCribe** command with the **BY** subcommand is used to determine the median for the values in each vertical strip.

```
MTB > describe c1;
SUBC> by c5.
```

	size	N	MEAN	MEDIAN	TRMEAN	STDEV	SEMEAN
price	0	4	90.50	92.50	90.50	8.89	4.44
	1	17	115.24	115.00	115.80	20.72	5.03
	2	11	158.82	151.00	158.56	27.32	8.24
	3	5	183.4	176.0	183.4	27.8	12.4
	4	2	190.00	190.00	190.00	9.90	7.00
	5	1	205.00	205.00	205.00	*	*

	size	MIN	MAX	Q1	Q3
price	0	78.00	99.00	81.50	97.50
	1	72.00	150.00	96.50	133.00
	2	121.00	199.00	139.00	190.00
	3	150.0	222.0	160.0	210.5
	4	183.00	197.00	*	*
	5	205.00	205.00	*	*

Below, the values of the medians and the midpoints of each interval are stored in columns C6 and C7. In the next section, we will create a median trace with the **MPLOt** command.

```
MTB > set c6
DATA> 92.50 115.00 151 176 190 205
DATA> set c7
DATA> 1250 1750 2250 2750 3250 3750
DATA> end
MTB > name c6 'medians' c7 'midpoint'
```

The MPLOt Command

This command is similar to the **PLOt** command, except **MPLOt** (M is for multiple) puts several plots on the same axes according to the following format:

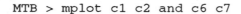

MPLOT C vs C, and C vs C,..., and C vs C

Up to 20 pairs of columns may be plotted. The first pair of columns is plotted with the letter A, the second with the letter B, etc. If several points fall on the same spot, a count is given as in **PLOT**. The command is illustrated below. Note that the letter B does not appear at the point that corresponds to 1750 square feet. This is because an A would also be printed at the same plotting location. The "2" indicates that two points are plotted in the same location. Lines connecting the medians can be drawn by hand.

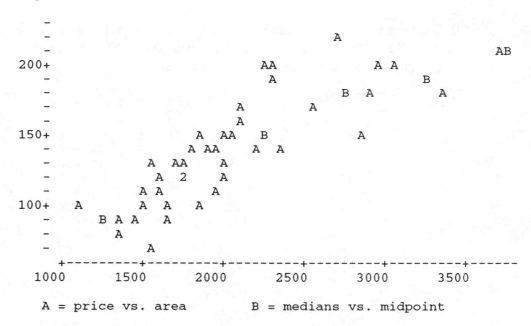

```
        MTB > mplot c1 c2 and c6 c7


        -
        -
        -                                     A
        -                                                            AB
  200+                            AA          A A
        -                          A                  B
        -                              B  A        A
        -                   A       A
        -                   A
  150+             A  AA  B         A
        -             A AA    A  A
        -         A  AA    A
        -           A  2    A
        -         A A      A
  100+   A      A  A    A
        -     B A A   A
        -       A
        -        A
        +---------+---------+---------+---------+---------+------
       1000     1500      2000      2500      3000      3500


        A = price vs. area        B = medians vs. midpoint
```

Side-by-side boxplots can also be used to examine the relationship between price and size of a house. Below we use the **BY** subcommand to draw individual boxplots of house prices for each category of size stored in C5.

```
MTB > boxp c1;
SUBC> by c5.

size
```

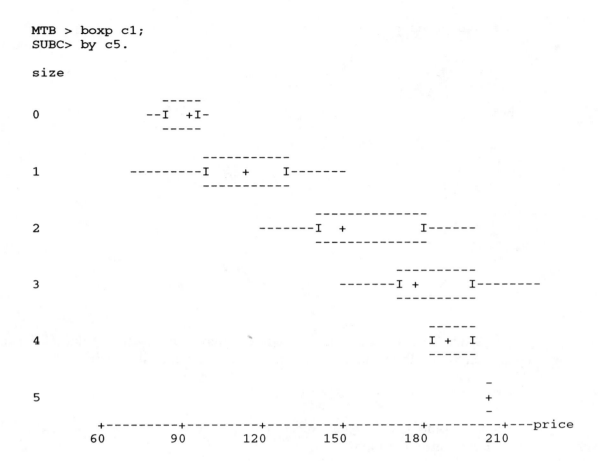

The REGRess Command

Example 2.6 of *I.P.S.* discusses the relationship between age and growth. The data are given in Table 2.3 of *I.P.S.* The data for the mean heights of the Kalama children have been entered into column C2 of KALAMA.MTW. The ages of the children have been entered into column C1. The following example shows the **PLOT** command being used to plot these data so that 'height' is on the vertical (*y*) axis and 'age' is on the horizontal (*x*) axis.

```
MTB > info

COLUMN     NAME       COUNT
C1         age          12
C2         height       12

CONSTANTS USED: NONE
```

```
MTB > plot c2 c1
```

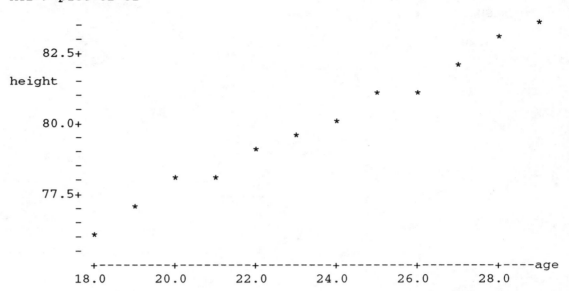

The Minitab **REGRess** command will calculate a least-squares line of the form $y = a + bt$ from data. The format for the **REGRess** command is

```
REGRess C on 1 predictor C
```

The first column is the y variable, or the variable that we want to predict (height). The second column is the predictor or t variable (age). The 1 indicates that only one predictor variable is being used and is not optional in this command. (In Chapter 10, we will consider using more than one predictor.) Below we illustrate the use of the **REGRess** command.

```
MTB > regress c2 1 c1

The regression equation is
height = 64.9 + 0.635 age

Predictor        Coef        Stdev      t-ratio          p
Constant      64.9283       0.5084       127.71      0.000
age           0.63497      0.02140        29.66      0.000

s = 0.2560      R-sq = 98.9%      R-sq(adj) = 98.8%

Analysis of Variance

SOURCE         DF           SS           MS          F          p
Regression      1       57.655       57.655     880.00      0.000
Error          10        0.655        0.066
Total          11       58.310

Unusual Observations
Obs.      age      height       Fit Stdev.Fit   Residual    St.Resid
   3     20.0     78.1000   77.6276    0.1052     0.4724       2.02R

R denotes an obs. with a large st. resid.
```

The above output indicates that the least-squares regression equation is height = 64.9 + 0.635 age. Below this equation, the output indicates that $a = 64.9283$ and $b = 0.63497$ are more accurate values of the regression parameters. These values are located under the column labeled Coef. Other useful information is provided and will be discussed later.

The fitted values (height = 64.9283 + 0.63497 age) and the residuals (residual = observation − fit) for the above regression can be obtained using the **LET** command and the least-squares regression equation. C2 contains the data for the response variable, 'height'; C1 contains the data for the explanatory variable, 'age'. The residuals from the regression can be calculated by first finding the fitted values using the regression equation, then subtracting those values from the actual observations:

```
MTB > let c3 = 64.9283 + 0.63497 * c1
MTB > let c4 = c2 - c10
MTB > name c3 'fits' c4 'resids'
MTB > print c3

fits
   76.3578    76.9927    77.6277    78.2627    78.8976    79.5326    80.1676
   80.8026    81.4375    82.0725    82.7075    83.3424

MTB > print c4

resids
-0.257759   0.007271   0.472298  -0.062675  -0.097633   0.167389  -0.267578
 0.297447  -0.237518  -0.272484   0.092545   0.157570
```

The residuals can also be obtained using the **RESIduals** subcommand with the following format:

```
RESIduals put into C
```

To store the residuals in C4, the **RESIduals** subcommand is used below. The output will be identical to that shown above, so it is not repeated. A residual plot is obtained by plotting the residuals versus age with the **PLOT** command.

```
MTB > regress c2 1 c1;
SUBC> residuals c4.
        .
        .   (same regression output as above)
        .
MTB > name c4 'resids'
MTB > plot c4 c1
```

```
     0.50+
        -                    *
  resids-
        -
        -                                              *
     0.25+
        -
        -                              *                              *
        -                                                       *
        -
     0.00+           *
        -                    *
        -                        *
        -
        -
    -0.25+ *                            *          *        *
        -
         +---------+---------+---------+---------+---------+------age
        18.0      20.0      22.0      24.0      26.0      28.0
```

The LOGTen Transformation*

Consider the oil production data from 1880 to 1972 given in Table 2.5 of *I.P.S* and in OIL.MTW.

```
MTB > print c1 c2
```

ROW	YEAR	PROD
1	1880	30
2	1890	77
3	1900	149
4	1905	215
5	1910	328
6	1915	432
7	1920	689
8	1925	1069
9	1930	1412
10	1935	1655
11	1940	2150
12	1945	2595
13	1950	3803
14	1955	5626
15	1960	7674
16	1962	8882

---

* This material is important in biology, business, and some other areas of application, but can be omitted without loss of continuity.

```
        17    1964    10310
        18    1966    12016
        19    1968    14104
        20    1970    16690
        21    1972    18584

   MTB > plot c2 c1


            -
    18000+                                                          *
            -                                                     *
     PROD   -
            -                                                  *
            -
    12000+                                                 *
            -                                            *
            -
            -                                         *
            -                                       *
     6000+                                       *
            -
            -                                 *
            -                          *    *
            -                  *    *    *
        0+        *      *     *    *    *
            ------+---------+---------+---------+---------+---------+---------+YEAR
               1880      1900      1920      1940      1960      1980
```

The oil production data displayed above appears to fit an exponential model. To check whether the growth is actually exponential, we will apply a logarithmic transformation and check whether the transformed data points lie along a straight line.

The LOGTen Command

Minitab's **LOGTen** command will find the logarithm to the base 10 of a constant or a column, then store the value into another constant or column. The command format is

```
LOGTen of E, put into E
```

Below we determine whether the log transformation results in a straight line, that is, whether oil production has exponential growth. This is done by first computing the logarithms of the data in C2 and storing them in C3 using the **LOGTen** command. To identify C3 as the logarithms, we name the column 'logs'. Finally, the **PLOT** command is used to check whether the logarithm grows linearly.

```
MTB > logt c2 c3
MTB > name c3 'log-oil'
MTB > plot c3 c1
```

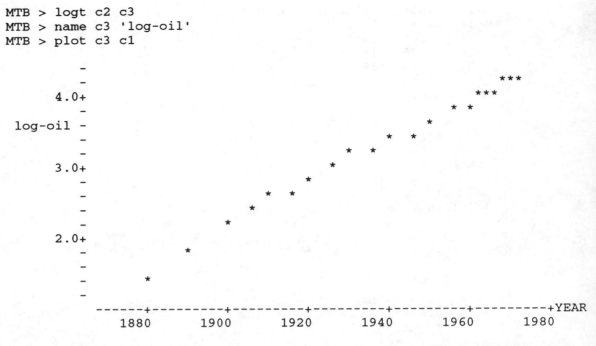

The above plot of the logarithms versus year shows that the transformation does result in a plot that is quite close to a straight line; hence the growth is exponential. A small deviation from the pattern occurred during the 1930s, when growth slowed during the Great Depression.

The same transformation could also have been computed using the **LET** command:

```
MTB > let c3 = logt(c2)
```

To obtain the least-squares equation for the log of oil production (log-oil) and time (YEAR), we used the **REGRess** command. Since we will later want to plot the residuals, we use the **RESIduals** subcommand.

```
MTB > regr c3 1 c1;
SUBC> resid c4.

The regression equation is
log-oil = - 52.7 + 0.0289 YEAR

Predictor        Coef        Stdev      t-ratio        p
Constant     -52.6859       0.8622       -61.11    0.000
YEAR         0.0288796    0.0004452        64.86    0.000

s = 0.05650      R-sq = 99.6%      R-sq(adj) = 99.5%

Analysis of Variance

SOURCE         DF          SS          MS         F        p
Regression      1      13.432      13.432   4207.12    0.000
Error          19       0.061       0.003
Total          20      13.492

Unusual Observations
Obs.     YEAR     log-oil       Fit Stdev.Fit   Residual    St.Resid
  1      1880      1.4771    1.6079    0.0279    -0.1307       -2.66R
  8      1925      3.0290    2.9074    0.0133     0.1215        2.21R

R denotes an obs. with a large st. resid.
```

Minitab calculates the prediction equation as

$$\texttt{log-oil = - 52.7 + 0.0289 YEAR}$$

Again, the slope (0.0289) and the *y* intercept (−52.7) are rounded off. Minitab lists these parameters more accurately in the table immediately below the prediction equation.

The multiplicative factor in the exponential model can be obtained by raising 10 to the power of the slope. This can be done using the **LET** command:

```
MTB > let k1=10**0.0288796
MTB > print k1
K1        1.06876
```

The above calculation shows that between 1880 and 1972 oil production increased on average 6.876% per year.

Below, the residuals from the above regression are named and plotted.

```
MTB > name c4 'resid'
MTB > plot c4 c1
```

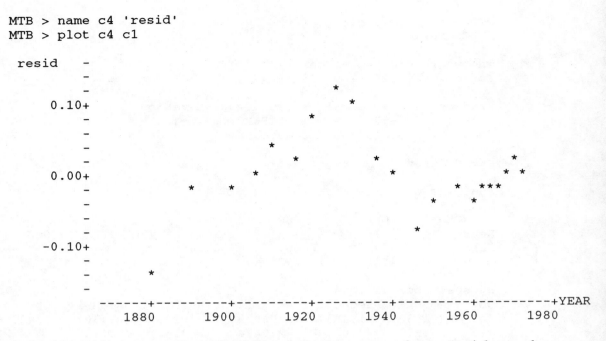

From the residuals, we can see deviations from the pattern of exponential growth. Oil production increased more rapidly than the average rate in the years 1900 to the beginning of the Great Depression. Production increased more slowly during the Depression and World War II. After the war, oil production returned to an above-average growth rate.

The CORRelate Command

The **CORRelate** command computes the correlation coefficient between two columns of data. If more than two columns are specified in the following format, Minitab will print a table giving the correlations between all pairs of columns.

```
CORRelate the data in C,...,C
```

Below we illustrate the use of the **CORRelate** command with data from Example 2.17 of *I.P.S.* The data represent the lengths in millimeters for a leg bone (femur) and a bone in the forearm (humerus) for five fossil specimens of *Archaeopteryx*. The data are given below and in FOSSIL.MTW.

```
MTB > retr 'fossil'
 WORKSHEET SAVED  6/29/1992

Worksheet retrieved from file: fossil.MTW
MTB > print c1 c2

  ROW   femur   humerus

    1      38        41
    2      56        63
    3      59        70
    4      64        72
    5      74        84

MTB > corr c1 c2

Correlation of femur and humerus = 0.994
```

The square of the correlation coefficient, r^2, appears in the output from the **REGRess** command. It is listed below as a percentage (R-sq = 98.8%).

```
MTB > regr c2 1 c1

The regression equation is
humerus = - 3.66 + 1.20 femur

Predictor       Coef       Stdev     t-ratio         p
Constant      -3.660       4.459      -0.82     0.472
femur        1.19690     0.07509      15.94     0.001

s = 1.982       R-sq = 98.8%      R-sq(adj) = 98.4%

Analysis of Variance

SOURCE         DF          SS          MS         F         p
Regression      1      998.21      998.21    254.10     0.001
Error           3       11.79        3.93
Total           4     1010.00
```

The **TABLe** Command

The **TABLe** command prints one-way, two-way, and multi-way tables. The format for the command is

```
TABLe the data classified by C,...,C
```

In the data set JOBS.MTW, we have stored the information about 120 job applicants for two departments. For each applicant, we have information about the sex, department of application, and the job offer decision. These are coded in C1 ('sex') as 0 = female and 1 = male. In C2 ('dept') the two departments are coded as 1 and 2. In C3 ('offer') the decision is coded as 1 = offered job, 0 = rejected.

```
MTB > info

COLUMN      NAME        COUNT
C1          sex           120
C2          dept          120
C3          offer         120

CONSTANTS USED: NONE
```

The **TABLe** command is conveniently used to determine the number of men and women that were offered jobs or rejected.

```
MTB > table 'sex' by 'offer'

ROWS: sex       COLUMNS: offer

              0         1       ALL

   0         40        25        65
   1         30        25        55
  ALL        70        50       120

  CELL CONTENTS --
                    COUNT
```

The **TABLe** command has a variety of subcommands available; more than one subcommand can be used at once. To obtain a list of possible subcommands the **HELP** command can be used. To obtain information about any of the subcommands, the **HELP** command can be used with the command and subcommand name. Below we use the **TABLe** command with the **ROWPercent** subcommand. If no subcommand is used, counts are provided by the **TABLe** command. After the table is printed, the cell contents are identified. In the table below, the cell contents are expressed as percents of the row values.

```
MTB > table 'sex' by 'offer';
SUBC> rowpercent.

ROWS: sex       COLUMNS: offer

              0         1       ALL

   0       61.54     38.46    100.00
   1       54.55     45.45    100.00
  ALL      58.33     41.67    100.00

  CELL CONTENTS --
                 % OF ROW
```

The two-way table above indicates that 41.67% of all applicants were offered jobs, but that only 38.46% of female applicants received job offers.

If three columns are specified in the **TABLe** command, three-way tables will be produced. These are essentially two-way tables for each value of the third variable specified. Below we examine three-way tables and see that department 1 offered jobs to one-half of all applicants (both male and female) while department 2 made job offers to only one-third of all applicants (both male and female). The difference in the overall job offer rates for males and females is due to the difference in the departments to which they applied. This is illustrated using the **TABLe** command with no subcommand.

```
MTB > table 'sex' by 'offer' by 'dept'

CONTROL: dept =  1
ROWS: sex        COLUMNS: offer

             0          1        ALL

  0         10         10         20
  1         20         20         40
ALL         30         30         60


CONTROL: dept =  2
ROWS: sex        COLUMNS: offer

             0          1        ALL

  0         30         15         45
  1         10          5         15
ALL         40         20         60


CELL CONTENTS --
              COUNT
```

EXERCISES

2.3   Vehicle manufacturers are required to test their vehicles for the amount of each of several pollutants in the exhaust. Even among identical vehicles the amount of pollutant varies, so several vehicles must be tested. The major pollutants in vehicle exhaust are hydrocarbons (HC), carbon monoxide (CO), and nitrogen oxides (NOX). EXHAUST.MTW gives data for these three pollutants for a sample of 46 light-duty engines of the same type. EN is an engine identifier. (Data taken from T. J. Lorenzen, "Determining statistical characteristics of a vehicle emissions audit procedure," *Technometrics,* 22 (1980), pp. 483-493.)

(a)   **PLOT** the relationship between carbon monoxide and nitrogen oxides. Describe the nature of the relationship. Is the association positive or negative? Is it nearly linear or clearly curved? Are there any outliers?

(b)   A writer on automobiles says, "When an engine is properly built and properly tuned, it emits few pollutants. If the engine is out of tune, it emits more of all important pollutants. You can find how badly a vehicle is polluting the air by measuring any one pollutant. If that value is acceptable, the other emissions will be OK." Do the data support this claim?

2.6   In 1974, the Franklin National Bank failed. Franklin was one of the 20 largest banks in the nation, and the largest ever to fail. Could Franklin's weakened condition be detected in advance by simple data analysis? The table below gives the total assets (in billions) and net income (in millions) for the 20 largest banks in 1973, the year before Franklin failed. Franklin is case number 19. The data are also given in BANKS.MTW. (Data from D. E. Booth, *Regression Methods and Problem Banks*, COMAP, Inc., 1986.)

Bank	1	2	3	4	5	6	7	8	9	10
Assets	49.0	42.3	36.6	16.4	14.9	14.2	13.5	13.4	13.2	11.8
Income	218.8	265.6	170.9	85.9	88.1	63.6	96.9	60.9	144.2	53.6

Bank	11	12	13	14	15	16	17	18	19	20
Assets	11.6	9.5	9.4	7.5	7.2	6.7	6.0	4.6	3.8	3.4
Income	42.9	32.4	68.3	48.6	32.2	42.7	28.9	40.7	13.8	22.2

(a)   We expect banks with more assets to earn higher income. **PLOT** the relationship between assets and income. Mark Franklin (bank 19) with a circle on your plot.

(b)   Describe the overall pattern of your plot. Are there any banks with unusually high or low income relative to their assets? Does Franklin stand out from other banks in your plot?

2.7   Do heavier cars cost more than lighter cars? CARS.MTW gives the base price in dollars and the weight in pounds for all 1991 model four-door sedans listed in an auto guide. Cars sold by American auto companies are coded with a "0" and foreign brands are plotted with a "1."

(a)   **PLOT** and describe the overall relationship between the weight of a car and its price. Is the association strong (weight and price closely connected) or weak? Is it generally positive or negative?

(b)   Use the **LPLOt** command to mark the foreign and domestic cars differently on a scatterplot. Describe the major differences between domestic and foreign cars as they appear in the plot.

2.8   The following table and LEAN.MTW give data on the lean body mass (kilograms) and resting metabolic rate for 12 women and 7 men who are subjects in a study of obesity. The researchers believe that lean body mass (that is, the subject's weight leaving out all fat) is an important influence on metabolic rate.

Subject	Sex	Mass	Rate	Subject	Sex	Mass	Rate
1	M	62.0	1792	11	F	40.3	1189
2	M	62.9	1666	12	F	33.1	913
3	F	36.1	995	13	M	51.9	1460
4	F	54.6	1425	14	F	42.4	1124
5	F	48.5	1396	15	F	34.5	1052
6	F	42.0	1418	16	F	51.1	1347
7	M	47.4	1362	17	F	41.2	1204
8	F	50.6	1502	18	M	51.9	1867
9	F	42.0	1256	19	M	46.9	1439
10	M	48.7	1614				

(a) Make a **PLOT** of the data for the female subjects. Which is the explanatory variable?

(b) Is the association between these variables positive or negative? What is the overall shape of the relationship?

(c) Now add the data for the male subjects to your graph, using the **LPLOt** command. Does the type of relationship that you observed in (b) hold for men also? How do the male subjects as a group differ from the female subjects as a group?

2.12 Thomas the cat is the subject of research on fleas. The researchers count the number of eggs produced each day by Thomas' flea population. Here are the counts for 27 consecutive days. The data are also provided in FLEA.MTW. (Data provided by Sayed Gaafar and Michael Dryden, Purdue University School of Veterinary Medicine.)

436	495	575	444	754	915	945	655	782
704	590	411	547	584	550	487	585	549
475	435	523	390	425	415	450	395	405

A median trace will help us see the pattern of change over time. Divide the data into periods of five consecutive days (discard the final two days) and calculate the median flea count for each period. This can be done with the following Minitab commands.

```
MTB > set c3
DATA> 5(1) 5(2) 5(3) 5(4) 5(5) 2(*)
DATA> end
MTB > desc c2;
SUBC> by c3.
```

Then use the **MPLOt** command to plot the individual counts against time (days 1 to 27) with the median trace added to the graph. Describe the pattern of change displayed by the trace.

2.32 One component of air pollution is airborne particulate matter such as dust and smoke. Particulate pollution is measured by using a vacuum motor to draw air through a filter for 24 hours. The filter is weighed at the beginning and end of the period and the weight gained is a measure of the concentration of particles in the air. In a study of pollution, measurements were made every 6 days with identical instruments in the center of a small city and at a rural location 10 miles southwest of the city. Because the prevailing winds blow from the west, it was suspected that the rural readings would be generally lower than the city readings, but that the city readings could be predicted from the rural readings. The table gives readings taken every 6 days between May 2 and November 26, 1986. The entry NA means that the reading for that date is not available, usually because of equipment failure. In the Minitab worksheet POLLUTION.MTW, these missing values are indicated with an asterisk (*). (Data provided by Matthew Moore.)

Rural	NA	67	42	33	46	NA	43	54	NA	NA	NA	NA
City	39	68	42	34	48	82	45	NA	NA	60	57	NA
Rural	38	88	108	57	70	42	43	39	NA	52	48	56
City	39	NA	123	59	71	41	42	38	NA	57	50	58
Rural	44	51	21	74	48	84	51	43	45	41	47	35
City	45	69	23	72	49	86	51	42	46	NA	44	42

To assess the success of predicting the city particulate reading from the rural reading, make a scatterplot of the 26 complete cases (both readings present) and find the least-squares regression line of the city reading y on the rural reading x. The **PLOT** and **REGRess** commands will not use observations with missing values.

(a)   Which observation appears to be the most influential? Is this the observation with the largest residual?

(b)   Locate in the table the observation you chose from the graph in (a) and compute its residual.

(c)   Do the data suggest that using the least-squares line for prediction will give approximately correct results over the range of values appearing in the data? (The incompleteness of the data does not seriously weaken this conclusion if equipment failures are independent of the variables being studied.)

(d)   On the fourteenth date in the series, the rural reading was 88 and the city reading was not available. What do you estimate the city reading to be for that date?

2.33   The calories and sodium content for each of 17 brands of meat hot dogs are given below and in HOTDOG.MTW.

Calories	173	191	182	190	172	147	146	139	175	136
	179	153	107	195	135	140	138			
Sodium	458	506	473	545	496	360	387	386	507	393
	405	372	144	511	405	428	339			

To delete the beef and poultry hotdogs from the Minitab worksheet, use the following commands.

```
MTB > delete 1:20 c1-c3
MTB > delete 18:34 c1-c3
```

(a)   Use the **PLOT** command to make a scatterplot of the amount of sodium in a hot dog of each brand versus the number of calories. Describe the main features of the relationship.

(b)   Compute two least-squares **REGRession** lines: one calculated using all of the observations, the other omitting the brand of veal hot dogs that is an outlier in both variables measured. Draw both regression lines on the scatterplot.

2.35 The following table and GAS.MTW give the results of a study of a sensitive chemical technique called gas chromatography, which is used to detect very small amounts of a substance. Five measurements were taken for each of four amounts of the substance being investigated. The explanatory variable x is the amount of substance in the specimen, measured in nanograms (ng), or units of 10^{-9} gram. The response variable y is the output reading from the gas chromatograph. The purpose of the study is to calibrate the apparatus by relating y to x. (Data from D.A. Kurtz (ed.), *Trace Residue Analysis*, American Chemical Society Symposium Series No. 284, 1985, Appendix.)

Amount (ng)	Response				
0.25	6.55	7.98	6.54	6.37	7.96
1.00	29.7	30.0	30.1	29.5	29.1
5.00	211	204	212	213	205
20.00	929	905	922	928	919

(a) **PLOT** the response versus amount for these data. Describe the relationship.

(b) Use the **REGRess** command with the **RESIduals** subcommand to compute the least-squares regression line of y on x, and plot this line on your scatterplot.

(c) Make a **PLOT** of the residuals against x. Describe carefully the pattern displayed by the residuals.

2.43 The following table and POP.MTW give the resident population of the United States from 1790 to 1980, in millions of persons:

Date	Pop.	Date	Pop.	Date	Pop.
1790	3.9	1860	31.4	1930	122.8
1800	5.3	1870	39.8	1940	131.7
1810	7.2	1880	50.2	1950	151.3
1820	9.6	1890	62.9	1960	179.3
1830	12.9	1900	76.0	1970	203.3
1840	17.1	1910	92.0	1980	226.5
1850	23.2	1920	105.7	1990	248.7

(a) **PLOT** population against time. The growth of the American population appears roughly exponential.

(b) Use the **LOGT** command to compute the base 10 logarithms of the population. **PLOT** the logarithms of population against time. The pattern of growth is now clear. An expert says that "the population of the United States increased exponentially from 1790 to about 1880. After 1880 growth was still approximately exponential, but at a slower rate." Explain how this description is obtained from the graph.

2.44   The number of motor vehicles (cars, trucks, and buses) registered in the United States grew as shown in the table below and in VEHICLES.MTW.

Year	Vehicles (millions)	Year	Vehicles (millions)
1940	32.4	1965	90.4
1945	31.0	1970	108.4
1950	49.2	1975	132.9
1955	62.7	1980	155.8
1960	73.9	1985	170.2

(a)   **PLOT** the number of vehicles against time.

(b)   Use the **LET** command to compute the logarithm of the number of vehicles and **PLOT** the logarithms against time.

(c)   Look at the years 1950 to 1980. Was the growth in motor vehicle registrations more nearly linear or more nearly exponential during this period? (Use a straightedge to assess the two graphs.)

(d)   Use the **REGRess** command with the **RESIdual** subcommand to find the least-squares line for the graph you chose in (c) as more linear. Use this line to approximately predict the number of vehicles registered in 1989. The actual number for 1989 was 183.7 million. Did your extrapolation over- or underpredict the true value?

(e)   Make a residual plot for 1950 to 1980. Are there any signs of systematic deviation from exponential growth?

2.48   A student wonders if people of similar heights tend to date each other. She measures herself, her dormitory roommate, and the women in the adjoining rooms; then she measures the next man each woman dates. Here are the data (heights in inches).

Women	66	64	66	65	70	65
Men	72	68	70	68	71	65

(a)   Make a **PLOT** of these data. Based on the scatterplot, do you expect the correlation to be positive or negative? Near ±1 or not?

(b)   Compute the **CORRelation** between the heights of the men and women.

(c)   Subtract 6 inches from the heights of all men given in the table. Recompute the **CORRelation** between the heights of the men and women. Does the correlation help answer the question of whether women tend to date men taller than themselves?

(d)   Use the **LET** command to enter heights for men that are exactly 3 inches taller than the women they date. What is the **CORRelation** between male and female heights?

2.65   The price of seafood varies with species and time. The following table and SEAFOOD.MTW give the prices in cents per pound received in 1970 and 1980 (PR70 and PR80) by fishermen and vessel owners for several species.

Species	PR70	PR80
Cod	13.1	27.3
Flounder	15.3	42.4
Haddock	25.8	38.7
Menhaden	1.8	4.5
Ocean perch	4.9	23.0
Salmon, chinook	55.4	166.3
Salmon, coho	39.3	109.7
Tuna, albacore	26.7	80.1
Clams, soft	47.5	150.7
Clams, blue, hard	6.6	20.3
Lobsters, American	94.7	189.7
Oysters, eastern	61.1	131.3
Sea scallops	135.6	404.2
Shrimp	47.6	149.0

(a)   **PLOT** the data with PR70 on the *x* axis and PR80 on the *y* axis.

(b)   Describe the overall pattern. Are there any points that lie away from the bulk of the data? If so, circle them on your graph. Are these unusual points outliers in the regression sense of having large residuals from a fitted line? Are they influential in the sense that removing them would change the fitted line? Or are they neither outliers nor influential?

(c)   Compute the **CORRelation** for the entire set of data.

(d)   What percent of the variation in 1980 prices is explained by the 1970 prices?

(e)   Recompute the **CORRelation** discarding the cases that you circled in (b). Do these observations have a strong effect on the correlation? Explain why or why not.

2.70   A survey of commercial poultry raising operations assessed the extent to which rodents are a problem in poultry houses. The operations surveyed were classified into two types (egg and turkey), and the extent of rodent infestation was classified as mild, moderate, or severe. The numbers of responses in each category are given in the following two-way table. The data are also provided in POULTRY.MTW. (Data from R. M. Corrigan and R. E. Williams, "The house mouse in poultry operations: pest significance and a novel baiting strategy for its control," *Proceedings of the Twelfth Vertebrate Pest Conference*, 1986, pp.120- 126.)

Type	Mild	Moderate	Severe
Egg	34	33	7
Turkey	22	22	4

(a)   Use the **TABLe** command with the **ROWPercents** subcommand to give the overall (marginal) percentages of mild, moderate, and severe infestations.

(b)   Give the percentages of each level of infestation for egg and for turkey operations separately. (These are the conditional distributions of the level of infestation, given the type of operation.)

2.77   Upper Wabash Tech has two professional schools, business and law. Here is a three-way table of applicants to these professional schools, categorized by sex, school, and admission decision. The data are also provided in WABASH.MTW. (Although these data are fictitious, similar though less simple situations occur in reality. See P. J. Bickel and J. W. O'Connell, "Is there a sex bias in graduate admissions?" *Science*, 187 (1975), pp. 398-404.)

	Business			Law	
	Admit	Deny		Admit	Deny
Male	480	120	Male	10	90
Female	180	20	Female	100	200

(a)   Make a two-way **TABLe** of sex by admission decision for the combined professional schools by summing entries in the three-way table. Use the following command.

```
MTB>  table c1 c2
```

(b)   Use the **ROWPercents** subcommand to compute separately the percents of male and female applicants admitted from your two-way table. Upper Wabash Tech's professional schools admit a higher percent of male applicants than of female applicants.

(c)   Now compute separately the percents of male and female applicants admitted by the business school and by the law school. Each school admits a higher percent of female applicants. Use the following commands.

```
MTB>  table c1 c2 c3;
SUBC>  rowp.
```

(d)   Explain carefully, as if speaking to a skeptical reporter, how it can happen that Upper Wabash appears to favor males when each school individually favors females.

2.81   The influence of race on imposition of the death penalty for murder has been much studied and contested in the courts. The following three-way table and PENALTY.MTW classify 326 cases in which the defendant was convicted of murder. The three variables are the defendant's race, the victim's race, and whether the defendant was sentenced to death. (Data from M. Radelet, "Racial characteristics and imposition of the death penalty," *American Sociological Review,* 46 (1981), pp. 918-927.)

	White defendant			Black defendant		
	Death penalty			Death penalty		
	Yes	No			Yes	No
White victim	19	132	White victim		11	52
Black victim	0	9	Black victim		6	97

(a)   Form a two-way **TABLe** of defendant's race by death penalty.

(b)   Show that Simpson's paradox holds: A higher percent of white defendants are sentenced to death overall, but for both black and white victims a higher percent of black defendants are sentenced to death.

(c)   Basing your reasoning on the data, explain why the paradox holds in language that a judge could understand.

2.93   What is the relationship between the number of home runs that a major league baseball team hits and its team batting average? On the one hand, we might expect better hitting teams to have both more home runs and higher batting averages. For individual players this is true: The correlation is about $r = 0.2$. On the other hand, teams have different styles of play and play their home games in different stadiums. Some may favor the home run, while other teams rely on singles and speed. The table below and BATTING.MTW give the data for American League teams in the 1990 season. Analyze the data and report your conclusions.

Team	Home runs	Batting average
Baltimore	132	.245
Boston	106	.272
California	147	.260
Chicago	106	.258
Cleveland	110	.267
Detroit	172	.259
Kansas City	100	.267
Milwaukee	128	.256
Minnesota	100	.265
New York	147	.241
Oakland	164	.254
Seattle	107	.259
Texas	110	.259
Toronto	167	.265

2.100   REGRESS.MTW contains three sets of bivariate data prepared by the statistician Frank Anscombe to illustrate the dangers of calculating without first plotting the data. The data are also given below. *All three sets have the same correlation and the same least -squares regression line* to several decimal places.

Data Set A

x	10	8	13	9	11	14	6	4	12	7	5
y	8.04	6.95	7.58	8.81	8.33	9.96	7.24	4.26	10.84	4.82	5.68

Data Set B

x	10	8	13	9	11	14	6	4	12	7	5
y	9.14	8.14	8.74	8.77	9.26	8.10	6.13	3.10	9.13	7.26	4.74

Data Set C

x	8	8	8	8	8	8	8	8	8	8	19
y	6.58	5.76	7.71	8.84	8.47	7.04	5.25	5.56	7.91	6.89	12.50

(a)   Calculate the **CORRelation** and the least-squares **REGRession** line for all three data sets and verify that they agree.

(b)   **PLOT** each of the three data sets and draw the regression line on each of the plots.

(c)   In which of the three cases would you be willing to use the fitted regression line to predict y given that $x = 14$? Explain your answer in each case.

2.102   We can explore in more detail the relation between calories and sodium in hot dogs. Data for three types of hot dogs are given in HOTDOG.MTW and in Table 1.4 (page 36) of *I.P.S.* The types are codes as 1 for beef, 2 for meat, and 3 for poultry.

(a)   Meat and beef hot dogs are quite similar. **DELEte** the data for poultry hotdogs and make a **PLOT** of sodium y against calories x. The meat hot dog data contain an outlier in x, a veal hot dog that has unusually few calories. Mark the point for this brand on your scatterplot. Does it appear that it will be influential when the regression line is fitted?

(b)   Compute the least-squares **REGRession** line of sodium on calories for all cases, and then for all cases except the veal hot dog marked in (a). Draw both lines on your scatterplot. Was the case noted highly influential?

(c)   Figure 1.11 in *I.P.S.* suggests that poultry hot dogs differ from the other types, at least in the distribution of calories. **RETRieve** the original HOTDOG worksheet and use the **LPLOt** command to make a new plot of sodium against calories, using different symbols for each type of hotdog. Describe the major differences (if any) in the calorie-sodium relationship for the two groups plotted.

(d)   Compute the least-squares **REGRession** line of sodium on calories for poultry hot dogs. Draw this line and the regression line for meat and beef hot dogs (with the outlier omitted) on your graph from (c). Give the r^2-values for both regressions. If the regression lines are used to predict sodium from calories, for which group of hot dogs will the prediction be more reliable? Would you be willing to use a single regression line to predict sodium from calories for all types of hot dogs?

2.104 Environmentalists, government officials, and vehicle manufacturers are all interested in studying the exhaust emissions produced by motor vehicles. The major pollutants in vehicle exhaust are hydrocarbons (HC), carbon monoxide (CO), and nitrogen oxides (NOX). EXHAUST.MTW and Table 2.9 (page 214) of *I.P.S.* give data for these three pollutants for a sample of 46 light-duty engines. The data is also given in Table 2.9 (page 214) of *I.P.S.* EN is an engine identifier. (Data taken from T. J. Lorenzen, "Determining statistical characteristics of a vehicle emissions audit procedure," *Technometrics,* 22 (1980), pp. 483-493.)

(a) Use the **PLOT** command to plot HC against CO, HC against NOX, and NOX against CO.

(b) For each plot, describe the nature of the association. In particular, which pollutants are positively associated and which are negatively associated?

(c) Inspect your plots carefully and circle any points that appear to be outliers or influential observations. Next to the circles, indicate the EN identifier. Does any consistent pattern of unusual points appear in all three plots?

(d) Use the **CORRelation** command specifying all three variables. The correlation will be calculated between every pair of variables. If you found unusual points, compute the correlations both with and without these points.

(e) Compute the least-squares **REGRession** lines corresponding to the three plots; use CO to predict HC and NOX, and NOX to predict HC.

(f) Compute the least-squares lines omitting the unusual points as a check on the influence of these points.

(g) Summarize the results of your analysis. In particular, is any of these pollutants a good predictor of another pollutant?

2.105 There are different ways to measure the amount of money spent on education. Average salary paid to teachers and expenditures per pupil are two commonly used measures. Table 2.10 in *I.P.S.* (page 215) and TEACHER.MTW give values for these variables by state and are based on information compiled by the National Education Association and reported in *The New York Times* on Nov. 8, 1986. The states are classified according to region: NE (New England), MA (Middle Atlantic), ENC (East North Central), WNC (West North Central), SA (South Atlantic), ESC (East South Central), WSC (West South Central), MN (Mountain), and PA (Pacific).

(a) Make a **STEMplot** or **HISTogram** for teachers' pay. Label any outlying cases with the state identifier. Do the same for spending per pupil. Do the distributions appear symmetric or skewed? Are the same states outliers in both distributions?

(b) Make a **PLOT** of pay *y* versus spending *x*. Describe the pattern of the relationship between pay and spending. Is there a strong association? If so, is it positive or negative? Explain why you might expect to see an association of this kind.

(c) On your plot, circle any outlying points found in (a) and any additional points that appear to be outliers or influential in the scatterplot. Label the circled points with the state identifier. Are the points found in (a) outliers from the overall relationship?

(d)   Compute the least-squares `REGRession` line for predicting pay from spending. You will need the residuals for the next exercise, so use the `RESIduals` subcommand. Graph the line on your plot. Give a numerical measure of the success of overall spending on education in explaining variations in teacher pay among states.

(e)   Repeat (d) excluding Alaska. Do any of your conclusions change substantially?

2.106   Continue the analysis of teachers' pay and education spending begun in the previous exercise by looking for regional effects. Group the states from TEACHER.MTW into four regions as follows:

- Northeast: NE and MA

- Heartland: ENC and WNC

- South: ESC, SA, and WSC

- Mountain/Pacific: MN and PA

(a)   Construct `BOXPlots` for education spending in the four regions using the same scales. For each region, label any outliers (points plotted individually in the modified boxplot) with the state identifier.

(b)   Repeat part (a) for teachers' pay.

(c)   Do you see important differences in spending and pay by region? Are the differences consistent for the two variables, that is, are regions that are high in spending also high in pay and vice versa?

(d)   Display the residuals by region using `BOXPlots` with the same scales. Draw a line across your plot at zero. Do the residuals appear to differ by region? Describe any patterns that are noteworthy.

2.107   Can college grade point average be predicted from SAT scores and high school grades? The CSDATA.MTW worksheet set contains information on this issue for a large group of computer science students. The data is described in the data appendix (page 792) of *I.P.S.* We will look only at SAT mathematics scores as a predictor of later college GPA, using the variables SATM and GPA from CSDATA. Make a scatterplot, obtain r and r^2, and draw on your plot the least-squares regression line for predicting GPA from SATM. Then write a brief discussion of the ability of SATM alone to predict GPA.

2.108   The WOOD.MTW worksheet originates in a study of the strength of wood products. The data is described in the data appendix (page 793) of *I.P.S.* The researchers measured the modulus of elasticity for each of the 50 strips of wood two times. If there is not a strong relationship between the two measurements, this means that the measurement process is not repeatable. In many fields the correlation is used to assess the strength of the relationship between measurements and is reported as the *reliability* of the measurement process.

(a)   **PLOT** the data with T1 on the x axis and T2 on the y axis. Describe the relationship. Why would you expect it to be linear and positive?

(b)   Calculate the **CORRelation**. Is this measurement process highly reliable?

(c)   We have two ways to calculate the least-squares regression line for predicting T2 from T1. First find the line using the **REGRession** command. Then find the means and standard deviations for T1 and T2 and use these numbers along with the correlation to find the slope of the least-squares line. Verify that both methods give the same slope.

2.109   We will investigate the effect of adding an unusual observation to the WOOD.MTW data set. Add the observation T1 = 1.6, T2 = 1.9 to the data set and make a scatterplot of T2 versus T1.

(a)   The new point is an outlier in regression. To confirm this, **REGRess** T2 on T1 and plot the residuals versus T1.

(b)   The new point is not an outlier in T1 alone and it is also not an outlier in T2 alone. Verify these statements by constructing **STEMplots**, **BOXPlots**, or normal quantile plots for both variables.

(c)   How does the new point change the regression equation? Find the equation with and without the new point. Plot both regression lines on your scatterplot. Is this point influential?

(d)   How does the new point change the correlation? Report the **CORRelation** with and without the new point.

2.110   Once again we will add an unusual observation to the WOOD.MTW data set. Add the observation T1 = 2.2, T2 = 1.2 to the original data set (do not keep the extra observation from the previous exercise).

(a)   The new point is somewhat extreme in T1 and T2 but it is not far away from other values of these variables. Verify these statements by constructing **STEMplots**, **BOXPlots**, and normal quantile plots for both T1 and T2.

(b)   Calculate the mean and standard deviation for T1 and T2 with and without the new point. Does the new point affect these summary measures substantially for either variable?

(c)   **PLOT** T2 versus T1 with the new data point included. Does the new point appear to be influential? Find the equation for the regression line of T2 on T1 both with and without the new point and draw both lines on your plot. Is the new point in fact influential?

(d)   Calculate the **CORRelation** with and without the new point. Does the new point change the correlation substantially?

Chapter 3
Producing Data

Commands to be covered in this chapter:

SAMPle K rows from C,...,C, put into C,...,C

SORT C [carry along C,...,C] put into C [and C,...,C]

LET (algebraic expression, complete on one line)

UNSTack (C,...,C) into (E,...,E),...,(E,...,E)

RANDom K observations into each of C,...,C

TALLy the data in columns C,...,C

The SAMPle Command

The **SAMPle** command can be used to select a simple random sample (without replacement) from a population. The format for the command is

    SAMPle K rows from C,...,C, put into C,...,C

The constant K designates the sample size. K may be any integer that is less than or equal to the size of the input column. The command selects K rows (without replacement) at random from the specified columns. The rows are sampled in random order. If rows are sampled from several columns at once, the same rows are selected from each.

Suppose that a sample of 40 is to be selected from a population of 1000 individuals for the purpose of conducting a survey. The following Minitab commands could be used to select the sample. For illustration, we will label the individuals with identification numbers from 1 to 1000. A consecutive list of integers following the **SET** command may be abbreviated using a colon. For example, 6:10 means 6, 7, 8, 9, 10. Below we enter the numbers 1 to 1000 into C1 and then select 40 individuals to be put into C2 using the **SAMPle** command.

```
MTB > set c1
DATA> 1:1000
DATA> end
MTB > sample 40 c1 c2
MTB > name c2 'sample'
MTB > print c2

sample
    722    753    439    929    738    723    446    212    413    139    178
    639    187    185    646    746    847    963    337    500    594    908
    733     32    806    936    490    554    491    955    809    899    556
    123    319    544    484    611    538    341
```

The identification numbers listed above refer to individuals in the population. Once a sample is selected, a population list is needed to determine which individuals are to be included in the sample and will be asked to answer survey questions.

The SORT Command

The samples above were selected in random order. It may be convenient to sort these numbers. This is easily done using the SORT command. The SORT command orders the data in a column in numerical sequence. The format for the SORT command is as follows:

```
SORT C [carry along C,...,C] put into C [and C,...,C]
```

The identification numbers for the individuals to be included in the above random sample (C2) can be sorted and put into another column (C3) using the command:

```
MTB > sort c2 c3
MTB > name c3 'sort'
MTB > print c3

sort
     32    123    139    178    185    187    212    319    337    341    413
    439    446    484    490    491    500    538    544    554    556    594
    611    639    646    722    723    733    738    746    753    806    809
    847    899    908    929    936    955    963
```

The second column specified in the SORT command can be the same as the first column specified. In this case, the sorted data would simply replace the unsorted data.

```
MTB > sort c2 c2
MTB > print c2

sample
     32    123    139    178    185    187    212    319    337    341    413
    439    446    484    490    491    500    538    544    554    556    594
    611    639    646    722    723    733    738    746    753    806    809
    847    899    908    929    936    955    963
```

Randomization in Experiments

The **SAMPle** command can also be used to randomly select treatment groups in an experiment. For example, if 25 experimental subjects are to receive new drug therapy and 25 subjects are to receive a placebo, the following commands could be used to select the subjects to receive the new drug.

```
MTB > set c1
DATA> 1:50
DATA> end
MTB > sample 25 c1 c2
MTB > name c2 'drug'
MTB > print c2

  drug
    30    37     7    16    19     2    23    20    47    34     1    38    10
    44    46    26     6    32    15    48    13     5    33    43    18
```

As above, the identification numbers listed refer to specific individuals. A list of subjects would be used to determine which subjects correspond to these identification numbers.

An alternative method of assigning treatments to subjects is to make a list of the treatments. This is conveniently done by using parentheses with the **SET** command to abbreviate a list of duplicate numbers. For example, 3(1,2,4) means 1, 2, 4, 1, 2, 4, 1, 2, 4 and (1,2,4)3 means 1, 1, 1, 2, 2, 2, 4, 4, 4. There should be no blanks between the repeat factor and the corresponding parentheses. In the list below, 0 refers to a placebo and 1 refers to the new drug. The list of treatments is randomized by using the **SAMPle** command with the sample size (K) equal to the column size (50).

```
MTB > set c2
DATA> 25(0) 25(1)
MTB > name c2 'treat'
MTB > print c2

treat
    0    0    0    0    0    0    0    0    0    0    0    0    0    0    0
    0    0    0    0    0    0    0    0    0    0    1    1    1    1    1
    1    1    1    1    1    1    1    1    1    1    1    1    1    1    1
    1    1    1    1    1

MTB > sample 50 c2 c2
MTB > print c2

treat
    1    0    0    1    1    1    0    1    1    1    0    1    0    1    1
    0    0    1    0    0    1    0    0    1    0    0    0    0    1    1
    0    1    1    0    0    1    0    1    0    1    1    1    0    0    1
    0    0    1    1    0
```

In the example above, subject 1 receives the new drug, subjects 2 and 3 receive the placebo, subjects 4, 5, and 6 receive the new drug, and so on.

The **SAMPle** command can also be used to select treatment groups for more complicated experimental designs. Consider, for example, an experiment with two factors, such as in Example 3.4 of *I.P.S.* Factor A has two levels and Factor B has three levels. If there are 18 subjects, then 3 subjects should be included in each of the 6 possible treatment groups. Below we create a Minitab worksheet listing the possible treatments and subject identification numbers. Parentheses are again used as an abbreviation for a repeat factor and a colon is used to abbreviate a list of integers.

```
MTB > set c1
DATA> 9(1) 9(2)
DATA> set c2
DATA> 3(1) 3(2) 3(3) 3(1) 3(2) 3(3)
MTB > set c3
DATA> 1:18
DATA> end
MTB > name c1 'factor A'
MTB > name c2 'factor B'
MTB > name c3 'subjects'
MTB > print c1-c3
```

ROW	factor A	factor B	subjects
1	1	1	1
2	1	1	2
3	1	1	3
4	1	2	4
5	1	2	5
6	1	2	6
7	1	3	7
8	1	3	8
9	1	3	9
10	2	1	10
11	2	1	11
12	2	1	12
13	2	2	13
14	2	2	14
15	2	2	15
16	2	3	16
17	2	3	17
18	2	3	18

The worksheet above illustrates the experimental design that will be used, that is, 3 subjects in each of 6 experimental groups. The assignment of subjects into groups can be randomized using the **SAMPle** command to randomly assign subjects to the 6 treatments. The command

```
MTB > sample 18 c3 c3
```

will randomly assign treatments to subjects.

```
MTB > print c1-c3

ROW   factor A   factor B   subjects

  1        1          1          3
  2        1          1          2
  3        1          1         17
  4        1          2          1
  5        1          2          7
  6        1          2         13
  7        1          3          4
  8        1          3          5
  9        1          3          8
 10        2          1         11
 11        2          1         14
 12        2          1         10
 13        2          2         15
 14        2          2         16
 15        2          2          6
 16        2          3         18
 17        2          3         12
 18        2          3          9
```

Note that the subjects are now arranged in a random order so that subjects 3, 2, and 17 are included in the first group (Factor A level = 1, Factor B level = 1), subjects 1, 7, and 13 are included in the second group (Factor A level = 1, Factor B level = 2), etc.

The UNSTack Command

This command separates one or more columns into several blocks of columns. For most applications, the subcommand SUBScripts is needed. The rows with the smallest subscript are stored in the first block, the rows with the second smallest subscript in the second block, and so on. If you do not use the subcommand, each row is stored in a separate block. The values in the subscripts column must be integers. The format for the command is

UNSTack (C,...,C) into (E,...,E),...,(E,...,E)

This command is useful for separating experimental units for a randomized block experimental design. Consider, for example, the randomized block design outline in Figure 3.2 of *I.P.S.* The blocks consist of male and female subjects, while the treatments are three therapies for cancer. The following worksheet contains subject identification numbers for 30 subjects in the first column and codes to identify the sex of the subject (1 = male, 2 = female) in the second column. The UNSTack command is used to separate the subjects into these two groups.

```
MTB > info

COLUMN     NAME        COUNT
C1         subject       30
C2         sex           30

CONSTANTS USED: NONE

MTB > print c1 c2

 ROW   subject    sex

   1        1       1
   2        2       2
   3        3       1
   4        4       2
   .        .       .
   .        .       .
   .        .       .
  29       29       1
  30       30       2

MTB > unstack 'subject' into c3 c4;
SUBC> subs 'sex'.
MTB > name c3 'male'
MTB > name c4 'female'
MTB > print c3 c4

 ROW    male   female

   1       1        2
   2       3        4
   3       6        5
   4       8        7
   5       9       11
   6      10       13
   7      12       15
   8      14       16
   9      17       20
  10      18       23
  11      19       24
  12      21       26
  13      22       27
  14      25       28
  15      29       30
```

Note that the male subjects (sex = 1) were stored in the first block and the female subjects were stored in the second block. To complete the experimental design, we list the treatments in C5 and then randomize the data in each block (C3 and C4).

```
MTB > set c5
DATA> 5(1) 5(2) 5(3)
DATA> end
MTB > name c5 'treat'
MTB > sample 15 c3 c3
MTB > sample 15 c4 c4
```

```
MTB > print c3-c5

ROW    male   female  treat

  1       8      16      1
  2       3      30      1
  3      29       4      1
  4       1      15      1
  5      19      26      1
  6       6      28      2
  7      22       7      2
  8      12       2      2
  9      21      27      2
 10      14      24      2
 11      18      20      3
 12      25      13      3
 13       9      23      3
 14      10       5      3
 15      17      11      3
```

The **SAMPle** command has randomly assigned subjects 8, 3, 29, 1, and 19 (males) and subjects 16, 30, 4, 15, and 26 (females) to treatment 1. The individuals assigned to treatments 2 and 3 can be read off the above worksheet listing.

The RANDom Command

The **RANDom** command is used to generate random numbers. The format for the command is

```
RANDom K observations into each of C,...,C
```

where K is the number of random numbers to be generated and C,...,C are the column(s) in which the random numbers are to be stored. If no subcommands are used, **RANDom** generates random numbers from the normal distribution, with a mean of 0 and a standard deviation of 1. This was illustrated in Chapter 1. Random numbers from a normal distribution with a different mean and standard deviation can be generated with the **RANDom** command with the following subcommand:

```
NORMal [mu = K [sigma = K]]
```

The command can also be used to generate a random sequence of 0s and 1s with the probability of selecting a 1 equal to *p*. This is done with the subcommand

```
BERNoulli trials with p = K
```

Consider a survey in which respondents are asked, "Did you, yourself, happen to buy groceries in the last 48 hours?" Suppose that you would like to simulate the responses of a simple random sample (SRS) of size 150 from a population with population proportion $p = 0.3$. This is done as follows:

```
MTB > random 150 c1;
SUBC> bern .3.
MTB > print c1

C1
    0    1    0    1    1    0    0    0    1    0    1    1    0    0    0
    0    1    0    0    1    0    0    0    0    0    0    0    1    1    0
    1    0    1    0    1    0    0    0    0    1    0    1    0    1    0
    0    0    1    1    0    0    1    0    0    0    1    1    0    0    1
    0    0    0    0    0    1    1    0    0    0    0    0    0    1    0
    1    0    0    1    0    1    0    0    1    1    1    0    0    0    1
    0    0    0    1    1    1    1    0    0    0    0    0    1    0    0
    0    0    1    0    0    0    1    1    0    1    0    0    1    1    0
    0    0    0    1    1    0    0    0    0    0    0    0    1    1    0
    0    1    1    0    0    0    1    0    0    1    0    0    1    1    0

MTB > mean c1
    MEAN     =      0.35333
```

The results above indicate that 53 people answered "Yes," 97 people answered "No," and the proportion of people answering "yes" was 0.35333. If the simulation was repeated, or another interviewer asked another 150 subject, the result would be slightly different. In the following example the proportion answering "Yes" is 0.28667.

```
MTB > random 150 c2;
SUBC> bern .3.
MTB > mean c2
    MEAN     =      0.28667
```

The **RANDom** command can also be used with several columns at a time to do repeated sampling. To generate 20 replications of the above sample, specify 20 columns in the command.

The **TALLy** Command

The **TALLy** command produces and prints tables for each column named in the following format:

```
TALLy the data in columns C,...,C
```

If no subcommand is used, the output will contain frequency counts for every distinct value in the input column. The columns must contain integers or missing values (*). The **PERCent** subcommand gives percentages for each distinct value in the input column(s), starting at the smallest distinct value. The **COUNts** subcommand gives frequency counts for each distinct value in each input column. This is the default action of **TALLy** if no subcommands are given. The **CUMCounts** subcommand gives cumulative frequency counts for each distinct value in the input column(s), starting at the smallest distinct value. The **CUMPercents** subcommand gives cumulative percentage values for each distinct value in the input column(s), starting at the smallest distinct value. The **ALL** subcommand produces all four of the **TALLy** distributions:

The **TALLy** command is useful for summarizing the results of several replications. Below, we generate 20 samples of size 150 and summarize the results using the **PERCents** subcommand.

```
MTB > random 150 c1-c20;
SUBC> bern .3.
MTB > tally c1-c20;
SUBC> percents.
```

C1	PERCENT	C2	PERCENT	C3	PERCENT	C4	PERCENT
0	68.00	0	67.33	0	71.33	0	74.00
1	32.00	1	32.67	1	28.67	1	26.00

C5	PERCENT	C6	PERCENT	C7	PERCENT	C8	PERCENT
0	71.33	0	72.67	0	73.33	0	72.67
1	28.67	1	27.33	1	26.67	1	27.33

C9	PERCENT	C10	PERCENT	C11	PERCENT	C12	PERCENT
0	71.33	0	68.67	0	64.67	0	62.00
1	28.67	1	31.33	1	35.33	1	38.00

C13	PERCENT	C14	PERCENT	C15	PERCENT	C16	PERCENT
0	62.00	0	71.33	0	60.67	0	65.33
1	38.00	1	28.67	1	39.33	1	34.67

C17	PERCENT	C18	PERCENT	C19	PERCENT	C20	PERCENT
0	67.33	0	65.33	0	72.00	0	72.00
1	32.67	1	34.67	1	28.00	1	28.00

To observe the variability of the SRSs, we can display the results of the 20 replications in a stemplot and describe the data. To do this, we first need to reenter the data.

```
MTB > set c1
DATA> .32 .3267 .2867 .26 .2867 .2733 .2667 .2733 .2867 .3133
DATA> .3533 .38 .38 .2867 .3933 .3467 .3267 .3467 .28 .28
DATA> end

MTB > stem c1

Stem-and-leaf of C1        N  = 20
Leaf Unit = 0.010

     4      2 6677
    10      2 888888
    10      3 1
     9      3 222
     6      3 445
     3      3
     3      3 889
```

```
MTB > desc c1

                N      MEAN    MEDIAN    TRMEAN     STDEV    SEMEAN
C1             20   0.31334   0.30000   0.31186   0.04154   0.00929

               MIN       MAX        Q1        Q3
C1         0.26000   0.39330   0.28000   0.34670
```

The 20 replications of SRSs of size 150 can be simulated more easily using the **RANDom** command with the **BINOmial** subcommand. The subcommand format is

```
BINOmial   n = K,  p = K
```

where n is the number of trials and p is the probability of success on each trial. In this example, $n = 150$ and $p = 0.3$. To find the values of $\hat{p}$, the results from the **RANDom** command are divided by the number of trials, 150.

```
MTB > random 20 c1;
SUBC> binomial 150 .3.
MTB > let c1 = c1/150
MTB > print c1

C1
   0.240000     0.306667     0.193333     0.306667     0.293333     0.340000
   0.366667     0.353333     0.220000     0.220000     0.360000     0.280000
   0.293333     0.280000     0.240000     0.240000     0.313333     0.326667
   0.313333     0.313333

MTB > stem c1

Stem-and-leaf of C1        N  = 20
Leaf Unit = 0.010

     1      1 9
     1      2
     3      2 22
     6      2 444
     6      2
    10      2 8899
    10      3 00111
     5      3 2
     4      3 45
     2      3 66

MTB > desc c1

                N     MEAN    MEDIAN    TRMEAN     STDEV    SEMEAN
C1             20   0.2900    0.3000    0.2911    0.0501    0.0112

               MIN      MAX        Q1        Q3
C1         0.1933   0.3667    0.2400    0.3233
```

The above stemplot looks different from the previous stemplot. This is because different random numbers are generated each time the **RANDom** command is used. The differences are not due to using two different methods of generating SRSs of size 150.

It is easier to see the distributions of the results in SRSs of size 150 if we examine a larger number of repetitions. Below we consider 100 repetitions.

```
MTB > random 100 c1;
SUBC> binomial 150 .3.
MTB > let c1 = c1/150
MTB > print c1

C1
   0.260000    0.280000    0.286667    0.200000    0.306667    0.286667
   0.360000    0.306667    0.280000    0.260000    0.306667    0.313333
   0.253333    0.273333    0.326667    0.286667    0.293333    0.286667
   0.360000    0.300000    0.333333    0.300000    0.273333    0.260000
   0.273333    0.253333    0.240000    0.360000    0.286667    0.306667
   0.280000    0.266667    0.186667    0.340000    0.306667    0.340000
   0.293333    0.273333    0.266667    0.326667    0.333333    0.313333
   0.300000    0.326667    0.400000    0.313333    0.306667    0.246667
   0.233333    0.293333    0.300000    0.246667    0.313333    0.266667
   0.360000    0.266667    0.326667    0.333333    0.273333    0.306667
   0.326667    0.346667    0.313333    0.393333    0.340000    0.253333
   0.320000    0.293333    0.340000    0.226667    0.286667    0.280000
   0.240000    0.266667    0.260000    0.273333    0.286667    0.300000
   0.360000    0.286667    0.306667    0.300000    0.340000    0.253333
   0.286667    0.180000    0.326667    0.380000    0.260000    0.333333
   0.246667    0.293333    0.326667    0.286667    0.346667    0.320000
   0.246667    0.293333    0.313333    0.313333

MTB > stem c1

Stem-and-leaf of C1          N  = 100
Leaf Unit = 0.010

      2    1 88
      3    2 0
      5    2 23
     15    2 4444445555
     31    2 6666666666777777
    (20)   2 88888888888888999999
     49    3 00000000000000001111111
     28    3 2222222223333
     15    3 4444444
      8    3 66666
      3    3 89
      1    4 0

MTB > desc c1

               N      MEAN    MEDIAN    TRMEAN     STDEV    SEMEAN
C1           100   0.29600   0.29333   0.29644   0.04039   0.00404

               MIN       MAX        Q1        Q3
C1         0.18000   0.40000   0.26833   0.32667
```

The distribution illustrated above is symmetric and appears to be normal, as was seen in Figure 3.4 of *I.P.S.* Below, a normal quantile plot is produced confirming that the sampling distribution is very close to normal.

```
MTB > nscores c1 c2
MTB > plot c2 c1
```

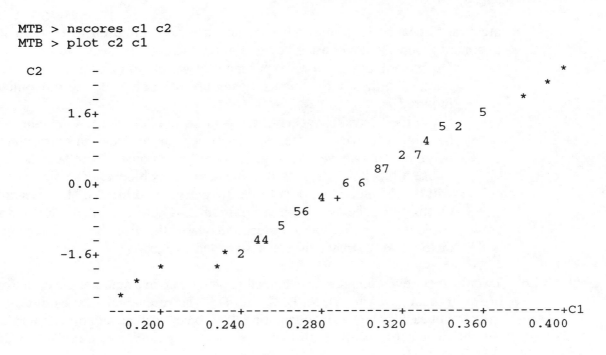

EXERCISES

3.16   You are testing a new medication for relief of migraine headache pain. You intend to give the drug to migraine sufferers and ask them 1 hour later to estimate what percent of their pain has been relieved. You have 40 patients available to serve as subjects. Their names are given below and in MIGRAINE.MTW.

(a)   Outline an appropriate design for the experiment, taking the placebo effect into account.

(b)   The names of the subjects are given below. Use the **SAMP1e** command to do the randomization required by your design. List the subjects to whom you will give the drug.

Abrams	Danielson	Gupta	Lippman	Rosen
Adamson	Durr	Gutierrez	Martinez	Solomon
Afifi	Duttman	Hwang	McNeill	Thompson
Brown	Edwards	Iselin	Morse	Travers
Cansico	Fluharty	Janle	Ng	Turing
Chen	Garcia	Kaplan	Obramowitz	Ullmann
Cranston	Gerson	Krushchev	Rivera	Williams
Curzakis	Green	Lattimore	Roberts	Wong

3.20   You decide to use a completely randomized design in the two-factor mathematics education experiment described in Example 3.4 of *I.P.S.* A mathematics education researcher wants to know whether it is better to present questions as motivation before the text passage or as a review after the passage. The result may depend on the type of question asked: simple fact, computation, or word problem. The researcher therefore prepares six versions of an instructional unit in elementary algebra. Because it is disruptive to assign school children at random to the treatment groups, you will use 12 classes of the same grade level instead.

(a)   Outline the design of an experiment in which you assign these classes at random to the six treatments. Then use Minitab to do the randomization required.

(b)   Six of the 12 available classes are in one school district and the other six are in another district. Differences between the districts, in curriculum and otherwise, may have a strong effect on the response. You therefore decide to use a block design with the two districts as blocks. The six treatments will be assigned at random to the six classes within each block separately. Outline the design with a diagram. Then use Minitab to do the randomization. Report your result in a table that lists the six classes in each district and the treatment you assigned to each class.

3.26   Twenty overweight females have agreed to participate in a study of the effectiveness of four reducing regimens, A, B, C, and D. The researcher first calculates how overweight each subject is by comparing the subject's actual weight with her "ideal" weight. The subjects and their excess weights in pounds are given below and in WEIGHT.MTW.

Birnbaum	35	Hernandez	25	Moses	25	Smith	29
Brown	34	Jackson	33	Nevesky	39	Stall	33
Brunk	30	Kendall	28	Obrach	30	Tran	35
Dixon	34	Loren	32	Rodriguez	30	Wilansky	42
Festinger	24	Mann	28	Santiago	27	Williams	22

The response variable is the weight lost after 8 weeks of treatment. Because the initial amount overweight will influence the response variable, a block design is appropriate.

(a)   Use the **SORT** command to arrange the subjects in order of excess weight. Use the **UNSTack** command to form five blocks by grouping the four least overweight, then the next four, and so on.

(b)   Use Minitab to do the required random assignment of subjects to the four reducing regimens separately within each block. Be sure to explain exactly which subjects get each of the four treatments.

3.33   A manufacturer of specialty chemicals chooses 3 from each lot of 25 containers of a reagent to be tested for purity and potency. The control numbers stamped on the bottles in the current lot are given below and in BOTTLES.MTW. Use the **SAMPle** command to choose an SRS of 3 of these bottles.

A1096	A1097	A1098	A1101	A1108
A1112	A1113	A1117	A2109	A2211
A2220	B0986	B1011	B1096	B1101
B1102	B1103	B1110	B1119	B1137
B1189	B1223	B1277	B1286	B1299

3.35   The people listed below and in STAT.MTW are enrolled in a statistics course taught by means of television. Use the **SAMPle** command to choose 6 to be interviewed in detail about the quality of the course.

Agarwal	Dewald	Hixson	Puri
Anderson	Fernandez	Klassen	Rodriguez
Baxter	Frank	Mihalko	Rubin
Bowman	Fuhrmann	Moser	Santiago
Bruvold	Goel	Naber	Shen
Casella	Gupta	Petrucelli	Shyr
Cote	Hicks	Pliego	Sundheim

3.36   Minitab has a long string of "random" numbers available. If Minitab always started at the beginning of the list, you would always get the same data. To avoid this, most computers use the time of day (in seconds or fractions of a second) to choose a "random" starting point in the string. The **BASE** command tells the random number generator where to start reading its list. The random number generator will continue reading from this point for the remainder of the Minitab session or until a new Base is set. This is used to repeat a sequence of random numbers. The command format is as follows.

```
BASE for the random data generators = K
```

(a)   Use the **BASE** command to select a particular starting place. Select a sample of 5 numbers from a list of 20. Repeat the **BASE** command with the same start and repeat the randomization. Notice that the same sample is selected.

(b)   To choose samples or do experimental randomization, you should not always begin at the same place. Why not?

3.38   A club contains 30 student members and 10 faculty members. The students are

Abel	Fisher	Huber	Moran	Reinmann
Carson	Golomb	Jimenez	Moskowitz	Santos
Chen	Griswold	Jones	Neyman	Shaw
David	Hein	Kiefer	O'Brien	Thompson
Deming	Hernandez	Klotz	Pearl	Utts
Elashoff	Holland	Liu	Potter	Vlasic

and the faculty members are

Andrews	Fernandez	Kim	Moore	Rabinowitz
Besicovitch	Gupta	Lightman	Phillips	Yang

The student and faculty names are given in CLUB.MTW. The club can send four students and two faculty members to a convention and decides to choose those who will go by random selection. Use the **SAMPle** command (twice) to choose a stratified random sample of 4 students and 2 faculty members.

3.39   A university has 2000 male and 500 female faculty members. The equal opportunity employment officer wants to poll the opinions of a random sample of faculty members. In order to give adequate attention to female faculty opinion, he decides to choose a stratified random sample of 200 males and 200 females. He has alphabetized lists of female and male faculty members.

(a)   Use the **SET** command to enter the numbers 1 to 2000 for the males and 1 to 500 for the females. Use the **SAMPle** command to select 200 males and 200 females.

(b)   Use the **SORT** command to put the selected males in consecutive order. Do the same for the selected females. This will make it easier to select the names from the alphabetized lists.

3.49   Let us illustrate the idea of a sampling distribution in the case of a very small sample from a very small population. The population is the scores of 10 students on an exam, given below and in SCORES.MTW.

Student	0	1	2	3	4	5	6	7	8	9
Score	82	62	80	58	72	73	65	66	74	62

The parameter of interest is the mean score, which is 69.4. The sample is an SRS of size $n = 4$ drawn from this population.

(a)   Use the **SAMPle** command to draw an SRS of size 4 from this population. Write the four scores in your sample and calculate the mean $\bar{x}$ of the sample scores. This statistic is an estimate of the population parameter.

(b)   Repeat this process 10 times. Make a histogram of the 10 values of $\bar{x}$. You are constructing the sampling distribution of $\bar{x}$. Is the center of your histogram close to 69.4? (Ten repetitions give only a crude approximation to the sampling distribution.)

3.50   An entomologist samples a field for egg masses of a harmful insect by placing a yard-square frame at random locations and examining the ground within the frame carefully. He wishes to estimate the proportion of square yards in which egg masses are present. Suppose that in a large field egg masses are present in 20% of all possible yard-square areas–that is, $p = 0.2$ in this population.

(a)   Use the **RANDom** command with the **BERNoulli** subcommand to simulate the presence or absence of egg masses in each square yard of an SRS of 10 square yards from the field. What proportion of your 10 sample areas had egg masses?

(b)   Use the **RANDom** command with the **BINOmial** subcommand to simulate 20 SRSs of size 10. What proportion of the square yards in each of your 20 samples had egg masses? Make a **STEM-and-leaf** diagram from these 20 values to display the sampling distribution of $\hat{p}$ in this case. What is the median of this distribution? What is its shape?

3.51 An opinion poll asks, "Are you afraid to go outside at night within a mile of your home because of crime?" Suppose that the proportion of all adult U.S. residents who would say "Yes" to this question is $p = 0.4$.

    (a)   Use the **RANDom** command with the **BERNoulli** subcommand to simulate the result of an SRS of 20 adults. Be sure to explain clearly which digits you used to represent each of "Yes" and "No." What proportion of your 20 responses were "Yes"?

    (b)   Use the **RANDom** command with the **BINOmial** subcommand to simulate 10 SRSs of size 20 from the same population. Compute the proportion of "Yes" responses in each sample. Find the mean of these 10 proportions. Is it close to $\hat{p}$?

3.61 A medical study of heart surgery investigates the effect of drugs called beta-blockers on the pulse rate of the patient during surgery. The pulse rate will be measured at a specific point during the operation. The investigators decide to use as subjects 30 patients facing heart surgery who have consented to take part in the study. You have a list of these patients, numbered 1 to 30 in alphabetical order.

    (a)   Outline in graphical form a completely randomized experimental design for this study.

    (b)   Use Minitab to carry out the randomization required by your design and report the result.

3.63 A university's financial aid office wants to know how much it can expect students to earn from summer employment. This information will be used to set the level of financial aid. The population contains 3,478 students who have completed at least one year of study but have not yet graduated. A questionnaire will be sent to an SRS of 100 of these students, drawn from an alphabetized list.

    (a)   Use the **SET** command to enter the numbers 1 through 3,478.

    (b)   Use the **SAMPle** command to select the students in the sample.

3.68 A chemical engineer is designing the production process for a new product. The chemical reaction that produces the product may have higher or lower yield, depending on the temperature and the stirring rate in the vessel in which the reaction takes place. The engineer decides to investigate the effects of combinations of two temperatures ($50°$ C and $60°$ C) and three stirring rates (60 rpm, 90 rpm, and 120 rpm) on the yield of the process. Two batches of the feedstock will be processed at each combination of temperature and stirring rate.

    (a)   How many factors are there in this experiment? How many treatments? Identify each of the treatments. How many experimental units (batches of feedstock) does the experiment require?

    (b)   Outline in graphic form the design of an appropriate experiment.

(c)   The randomization in this experiment determines the order in which batches of the feedstock will be processed according to each treatment. Use Minitab to carry out the randomization. Clearly state the results.

3.72   To demonstrate how randomization reduces confounding, consider the nutrition experiment described in Example 3.7 of *I.P.S.* Suppose that the 30 rats are labeled 01 to 30. Suppose also that, unknown to the experimenter, the 10 rats labeled 01 to 10 have a genetic defect that will cause them to grow more slowly than normal rats. If the experimenter simply put rats 01 to 15 in the experimental group and rats 16 to 30 in the control group, this lurking variable will bias the experiment against the new food product. Use Minitab to assign 15 rats at random to the experimental group. Record how many of the 10 rats with genetic defects are placed in the experimental group and how many are in the control group. Repeat the randomization until you have done five random assignments. What is the mean number of genetically defective rats in experimental and control groups in your five repetitions?

3.74   (a)   Use the **RANDom** command with the **BINOmial** subcommand to draw 100 samples of size $n = 50$ from a population with $p = 0.6$. Use the **LET** command to calculate the value of $\hat{p}$ for each sample. Prepare a frequency **HISTogram** of the $\hat{p}$-values for each simulation.

(b)   Draw 100 samples each of sizes $n = 200$ and $n = 800$ from the same population. Prepare a frequency **HISTogram** of the $\hat{p}$-values for each simulation, using the same scales so that the three graphs can be compared easily. How does increasing the size of an SRS affect the sampling distribution of $\hat{p}$?

Chapter 4
Probability: The Study of Randomness

Commands to be covered in this chapter:

SUM the values in C [put sum into K]

SQRT of E, put into E

RANDom K observations into each of C,...,C

The SUM and SQRT Commands

In this chapter we will study the effect of randomness by considering the following dice game. The game costs one dollar to play. To begin, you roll a pair of dice. The possible outcomes are the sums 2 through 12. If you roll either a 7 or an 11, then you win two dollars. If you roll a 2, 3, or 12, then the outcome is called "craps" and you win nothing. If your roll has any other value (4, 5, 6, 8, 9, or 10), then you win the small amount shown in the table below. Note that for these outcomes, your winning is less than the cost of playing the game! The table below also provides the probability for each possible roll for a pair of dice.

Roll	2	3	4	5	6	7	8	9	10	11	12
Prob	$\frac{1}{36}$	$\frac{2}{36}$	$\frac{3}{36}$	$\frac{4}{36}$	$\frac{5}{36}$	$\frac{6}{36}$	$\frac{5}{36}$	$\frac{4}{36}$	$\frac{3}{36}$	$\frac{2}{36}$	$\frac{1}{36}$
Win	0	0	0.67	0.80	0.91	2	0.91	0.80	0.67	2	0

We have stored the above information in a Minitab worksheet, CRAPS.MTW. For each value of 'roll' stored in C1, the appropriate values for the probability and the amount that would be won are stored in C2 and C3, respectively.

```
MTB > info

COLUMN    NAME       COUNT
C1        roll       11
C2        prob       11
C3        winning    11

CONSTANTS USED: NONE
```

If X is a discrete random variable taking on the values $x_1, x_2, \ldots, x_k$ with probabilities $p_1, p_2, \ldots, p_k$, then the mean value of X is given by

$$\mu_x = x_1 p_1 + x_2 p_2 + \cdots + x_k p_k$$

We can use Minitab to compute the mean of a discrete distribution with the **LET** and **SUM** commands. The format of the **SUM** command is

```
SUM the values in C [put sum into K]
```

Below we store the values of $x_1 p_1, x_2 p_2, \ldots, x_k p_k$ in C15 and then use the **SUM** command to compute the mean. The result is stored in K1.

```
MTB > let c15 = c2*c3
MTB > sum c15 k1
   SUM    =       0.98667
```

Note that the mean winning in the above game is 0.98667, a value that is slightly less than one dollar, the cost of playing the game.

If X is a discrete random variable taking values $x_1, x_2, \ldots, x_k$ with probabilities $p_1, p_2, \ldots, p_k$, the variance of X is given by

$$\sigma_x = (x_1 - \mu_x)^2 p_1 + (x_2 - \mu_x)^2 p_2 + \cdots + (x_k - \mu_x)^2 p_k$$

The standard deviation σ_x of X is the square root of the variance. Both the variance and the standard deviation of a random variable can be computed using Minitab. The variance is computed by first storing the values of $(x_i - \mu_x)^2 p_i$ in C15 and then using the **SUM** command to compute the variance. The result is stored in K2.

```
MTB > let c15 = c2*(c3-k1)**2
MTB > sum c15 k2
   SUM    =       0.36244
```

The standard deviation is computed using the **SQRT** command. The command calculates square roots and has the following format.

```
SQRT of E, put into E
```

If you take the square root of a negative number, the answer is set equal to *, the missing value code, and the message "VALUE OUT OF BOUNDS" is printed. Note that variances and standard deviations are always positive.

```
MTB > sqrt k2 k3
   ANSWER =          0.6020
```

The mean and the variance could also be calculated using only the **LET** command with **SUM** as a function. This is illustrated below.

```
MTB > let k1 = sum(c2*c3)
MTB > print k1
K1       0.986667
MTB > let k2 = sum(c2*(c3-k1)**2)
MTB > print k2
K2       0.362444
```

Below we consider playing the dice game described above for five dollars instead of one. In C4, we will store the net return (including the original wager) from playing this game. The net return is obtained by a linear transformation: $y^* = -5 + 5x$, where x is the winning from a one-dollar game (stored in C3) and y^* is the net return from a five dollar game (to be stored in C4). After storing the values in C4 and naming the column, the mean and the variance of the distribution are obtained as above.

```
MTB > let c4 = -5+5*c3
MTB > name c4 'return5'
MTB > let k4 = sum(c2*c4)
MTB > print k4
K4       -0.0666668
MTB > let k5 = sum(c2*(c4-k4)**2)
MTB > print k5
K5       9.06111
```

The standard deviation is obtained by finding the square root of the variance.

```
MTB > sqrt k5 k6
K6       3.01017
```

Alternatively, the mean and variance could be found using the rules for means and variances of linear transformations:

$$\mu_{a+bX} = a + b\mu_X$$
$$\sigma^2_{a+bX} = b^2 \sigma^2_X$$

```
MTB > let k4 = -5 + 5*k1
MTB > print k4
K4       -0.0666668

MTB > let k5 = k2*5**2
MTB > print k5
K5       9.06111
```

Note that these are exactly the same as the mean and variance obtained above.

The RANDom Command

The RANDom command generates K random observations, from the distribution specified in the subcommand, into each of the columns specified in the following format.

```
RANDom K observations into each of C,...,C
```

In previous chapters, we used the **RANDom** command to generate observations with Bernoulli, binomial, and normal distributions. The **DISCrete** subcommand allows us to specify a discrete distribution. The values and corresponding probabilities are put into two columns and the following subcommand format is used to generate a random sample of 50 observations.

```
DISCrete distribution with x values in C, probabilities in C
```

Any discrete distribution can be specified by putting the values and corresponding probabilities into two columns. For example, to simulate 50 observations from a distribution with values −1, 0, and 1 and corresponding probabilities 0.2, 0.5, and 0.3, you would first enter these values into two separate columns and then generate random data by referring to these columns. For example,

```
MTB > READ C10 C11
DATA> -1 .2
DATA> 0 .5
DATA> 1 .3
DATA> END
MTB > RANDOM 50 C1;
SUBC> DISCRETE C10 C11.
```

Below we simulate 50 observations into C5 from the distribution of net returns that are stored in C4, with probabilities in C2. Then we use the **DESCribe** command so that we can see how close the mean and standard deviation of the simulated values are to the theoretical values computed above ($\mu_X = -0.666661$ and $\sigma_X = 3.01017$). We also use the **HISTogram** command to examine the shape of the distribution.

```
MTB > random 50 c5;
SUBC> disc c4 c2.
MTB > name c5 'rand5'
MTB > describe c5
```

	N	MEAN	MEDIAN	TRMEAN	STDEV	SEMEAN
rand5	50	0.150	-0.450	0.170	2.810	0.397

	MIN	MAX	Q1	Q3
rand5	-5.000	5.000	-1.163	-0.450

```
MTB > hist c5

Histogram of rand5    N = 50

Midpoint   Count
     -5        3   ***
     -4        0
     -3        0
     -2        9   *********
     -1       10   **********
      0       17   *****************
      1        0
      2        0
      3        0
      4        0
      5       11   ***********
```

The net returns from the first 10 bets were −5.00, −1.65, 5.00, 5.00, −1.00, −1.65, −0.45, −1.00, 5.00, and 5.00. If we average these values, we obtain 0.925. As we average the net returns from additional bets, the law of large numbers says that the average will tend to the mean of the net winnings distribution. The average value from all 50 simulations was 0.150, closer to the mean of the net winnings distribution (−0.0666661). However, we do see that although the mean of the net winnings distribution is negative, the outcome from the 50 simulations above indicates that the average winning was positive. This happens by chance. Similarly, the simulated value for the standard deviation, 2.81, is slightly lower than the above calculated value of 3.01. If the simulation was repeated, the new results would probably be slightly different.

Below we will examine the winnings from $10 and $15 bets, and then the sum and the difference of these bets. In C6 and C7, we save the winnings from rolls in $10 and $15 games.

```
MTB > let c6 = 10*c3
MTB > let c7 = 15*c3
MTB > name c6 'win10' name c7 'win15'
```

Using the values stored in C6 and C7, and the probabilities stored in C2, we next generate a sample of size 50 from these distributions and use the **DESCribe** command to examine the results.

```
MTB > random 50 c8;
SUBC> disc c6 c2.
MTB > random 50 c9;
SUBC> disc c7 c2.
MTB > name c8 'ranw10' c9 'ranw15'
MTB > desc c8 c9
```

	N	MEAN	MEDIAN	TRMEAN	STDEV	SEMEAN
ranw10	50	9.758	8.000	9.725	6.132	0.867
ranw15	50	15.88	13.65	16.00	9.66	1.37

	MIN	MAX	Q1	Q3
ranw10	0.000	20.000	6.700	9.100
ranw15	0.00	30.00	10.05	30.00

If we call the winning from a \$10 game X, and the winning from a \$15 game Y, then we can use the following rules:

$$\mu_{X+Y} = \mu_X + \mu_Y$$

$$\mu_{X-Y} = \mu_X - \mu_Y$$

$$\sigma^2_{X+Y} = \sigma^2_X + \sigma^2_Y$$

$$\sigma^2_{X-Y} = \sigma^2_X + \sigma^2_Y$$

The last two rules apply because X and Y are independent. Using these rules, we can determine that $\mu_{X+Y} = 24.6667$, $\mu_{X-Y} = -4.93333$, $\sigma^2_{X+Y} = \sigma^2_{X-Y} = 96.3500$,   and $\sigma_{X+Y} = \sigma_{X-Y} = 9.8151$.

```
MTB > let c10 = 'ranw10' + 'ranw15'
MTB > name c10 'sum'
MTB > let c11 = 'ranw15' - 'ranw10'
MTB > name c11 'diff'
MTB > desc c10 c11
```

	N	MEAN	MEDIAN	TRMEAN	STDEV	SEMEAN
sum	50	24.34	21.10	24.31	10.79	1.53
diff	50	-4.63	-4.00	-4.84	9.95	1.41

	MIN	MAX	Q1	Q3
sum	0.00	50.00	18.70	33.65
diff	-23.30	20.00	-7.71	-0.95

Note that the simulated values are close to but not exactly equal to the calculated theoretical values.

The UNIForm Subcommand

The **RANDom** command can be used to simulate observations from continuous distributions. Recall that in Chapter 1, we used the **RANDom** command with the **NORMal** subcommand to generate observations from a normal distribution. To generate random numbers that are spread out uniformly between two numbers, the following subcommand format is used with the **RANDom** command.

```
UNIForm  [continuous on a=K to b=K]
```

The uniform distribution covers the interval from a to b. If you omit the arguments, then $a = 0$ and $b = 1$ are used. Below, we let $a = 5$ and $b = 10$ and generate 200 observations from the uniform distribution.

```
MTB > random 200 c1;
SUBC> unif 5 10.
MTB > hist c1

Histogram of C1   N = 200

Midpoint    Count
     5.0       44   *********
     5.5      113   **********************
     6.0      112   **********************
     6.5       97   *******************
     7.0       97   *******************
     7.5       95   ******************
     8.0       93   ******************
     8.5      100   *******************
     9.0       81   ****************
     9.5      112   **********************
    10.0       56   ***********
```

EXERCISES

4.32   Choose an American household at random and let the random variable X be the number of persons living in the household. If we ignore the few households with more than seven inhabitants, the probability distribution of X is as follows. The distribution is also provided in SIZE.MTW.

Outcome	1	2	3	4	5	6	7
Probability	.240	.322	.177	.155	.067	.024	.015

(a)   Use the **SUM** command to verify that this is a legitimate discrete probability distribution.

(b)   Use the **RANDom** command with the **DISCrete** subcommand to simulate the family sizes of 100 families.

(c)   Make a **HISTogram** of the simulated values. Use the **TALLy** command to summarize the results of your simulation. Are your results consistent with the probability distribution?

(d)   Use the **LET** command to find the mean and standard deviation of the number of people living in a household. Use the **DESCribe** command to find these measures for the simulated familes. Compare the results.

4.33   A study selected a sample of children who were then in fifth grade and recorded how many years of school they eventually completed. Let X be the highest year of school that a randomly chosen fifth grader completes. (Students who go on to college are included in the outcome $X = 12$.) The probability distribution of X is given in FIFTH.MTW and below.

x_i	4	5	6	7	8	9	10	11	12
p_i	.010	.007	.007	.013	,032	.068	.070	.041	.752

(a)   Use the **SUM** command to verify that this is a legitimate discrete probability distribution.

(b)   Use the **RANDom** command with the **DISCrete** subcommand to simulate the education level achieved by 100 fifth graders.

(c)   Make a **HISTogram** of the simulated values. Use the **TALLy** command to summarize the results of your simulation. Are your results consistent with the probability distribution?

(d)   Repeat the simulation twice more. Do the results vary with each simulation?

4.37   Let X be a random number between 0 and 1 produced by the idealized uniform random number generator. We can use simulation to approximate probabilities. Use the **RANDom** command with the **UNIForm** subcommand to simulate 100 values. Make a **STEM-and-leaf** diagram of the simulated values. Use the results to approximate the following probabilities.

(a) $P(0 \leq X \leq 0.4)$

(b) $P(0.4 \leq X \leq 1)$

(c) $P(0.3 \leq X \leq 0.5)$

4.41   The random variable X has the standard normal $N(0,1)$ distribution. Use the **CDF** command (described in Chapter 1) to find each of the following probabilities.

(a) $P(-1 \leq X \leq 1)$

(b) $P(1 \leq X \leq 2)$

(c)   Simulate 100 observations from a standard normal $N(0,1)$ distribution using the **RANDom** command. (No subcommand is needed.) Make a **STEM-and-leaf** diagram of the 100 observations and use the result to estimate the probabilities in (a) and (b). Compare the estimates with the exact probabilities.

4.63   In a process for manufacturing glassware, glass stems are sealed by heating them in a flame. The temperature of the flame varies a bit. Here is the distribution of the temperature X measured in degrees Celsius.

Temperature	540°	545°	550°	555°	560°
Probability	.1	.25	.3	.25	.1

(a)   Enter the data into a Minitab worksheet. Use the **LET** command to find the mean temperature μ_X and the standard deviation σ_X.

(b)   Simulate 40 temperature measurements using the **RANDom** command with the **DISCrete** subcommand. Use the **DESCribe** command to find the means and standard deviations of the simulated values. Are they close to the values computed in (a)?

(c)   A manager asks for results in degrees Fahrenheit. The conversion of X into degrees Fahrenheit is given by

$$Y = \tfrac{9}{5}X + 32$$

Use the **LET** command to change the temperature distribution to Fahrenheit and then find the mean μ_Y and standard deviation σ_Y of the temperature of the flame in the Fahrenheit scale.

(d)   Use the **LET** command to convert the simulated values to Fahrenheit. Compute the mean and standard deviation using the **DESCribe** command.

4.88   Rotter Partners is planning a major investment. The amount of profit X is uncertain but a probabilistic estimate gives the following distribution (in millions of dollars):

Profit	1	1.5	2	4	10
Probability	.1	.2	.4	.2	.1

(a)   Enter the data into a Minitab worksheet. Use the **LET** command to find the mean profit and the standard deviation of the profit.

(b)   Rotter Partners owes its source of capital a fee of $200,000 plus 10% of the profits X. So the firm actually retains

$$Y = .9X - .2$$

from the investment. Use the **LET** command to find the mean and standard deviation of Y.

4.102   The distribution of colors of plain M&M candies is given in CANDY.MTW and below.

Color	Brown	Red	Yellow	Green	Orange	Tan
Probability	.3	.2	.2	.1	.1	.1

(a)   A small bag contains 25 M&Ms. Assign numbers to each color, such as $1 =$ Brown, $2 =$ Red, etc., and then simulate the contents of 10 bags using the **RANDom** command and **DISCrete** subcommand. Record the number of candies of each color in each of the bags.

(b)   What was the overall proportion of orange candies in your data? Was the observed proportion close to the probability, which is 0.1?

(c)   What was the mean number of orange candies in the bags? The theoretical mean is $\mu = 2.5$. Was the observed mean close to the theoretical value?

(d)   How many bags contained no orange candies? Do you expect bags of 25 M&Ms to often, sometimes, or almost never contain no orange candies?

4.103   Toss a balanced coin 10 times. What is the probability of a run of 3 or more consecutive heads? What is the distribution of the length of the longest run of heads? What is the mean length of the longest run of heads? These are quite difficult questions if we must rely on mathematical calculations of probability. Computer simulation of the probability model can provide approximate answers.

(a)   First, simulate 50 repetitions of tossing a balanced coin 10 times. Here are the Minitab commands that place the results of 10 tosses in each of columns 1 to 50; heads are represented by 1s and tails by 0s.

```
MTB > RANDOM 10 C1-C50;
SUBC> BERNOULLI .5.
MTB > PRINT C1-C50
```

(b)   Examine your 50 repetitions and record the length of the longest run of heads (1s) in each trial.

(c)   Make a table of the (approximate) probability distribution of the length X of the longest run of heads in 10 coin tosses. (The relative frequency of each outcome in many repetitions is approximately equal to its probability.) Draw a probability histogram of this distribution.

(d)   What is your estimate of the probability of a run of 3 or more heads?

(e)   Use the **LET** command to find the mean from your table of probabilities in (a). Then use the **DESCribe** command to find the average of the 50 values of X in your 50 repetitions. How close to the mean was the average obtained in 50 repetitions?

Chapter 5
From Probability to Inference

Commands to be covered in this chapter:

```
PDF for values in E [store results in E]
CDF for values in E [store results in E]
RANDom K observations into each of C,...,C
RMEAn E,...,E put mean of each row into C
ICHArt for C,...,C
XBARchart for C,...,C, subgroups are in E
```

The PDF Command

The **PDF** (probability distribution function) command has a special capability when used with the subcommand **BINOmial**. If no arguments are specified on the **PDF** command line, then the probability distribution of that binomial distribution will be printed. For example, below we obtain the probability of each possible outcome for a binomial distribution with $n = 10$ and $p = 0.1$.

```
MTB > pdf;
SUBC> binomial n=10 p=.1.

    BINOMIAL WITH N =  10  P = 0.100000
      K            P(X = K)
      0             0.3487
      1             0.3874
      2             0.1937
      3             0.0574
      4             0.0112
      5             0.0015
      6             0.0001
      7             0.0000
```

Note that for $K = 7$, $P(X = K)$ is equal to 0 (rounded to 4 decimal places). For $K = 8$, 9, and 10, $P(X = K)$ is also equal to 0, so these rows are not printed in the table of probabilities for the binomial.

The CDF Command

In addition to the **PDF** command, the **CDF** (cumulative distribution function) command also can be used to print a table of probabilities for the binomial distribution. The difference is that this command gives cumulative probabilities, that is, the probability that X is less than or equal to a value. Below we use Minitab to obtain the cumulative probabilities for a binomial with $n = 10$ and $p = 0.1$.

```
MTB > cdf;
SUBC> binomial n=10 p=.1.

    BINOMIAL WITH N =  10   P = 0.100000
      K  P( X LESS OR = K)
      0            0.3487
      1            0.7361
      2            0.9298
      3            0.9872
      4            0.9984
      5            0.9999
      6            1.0000
```

The probability that X is less than or equal to 7, 8, 9, or 10 is equal to 1, so these rows are not printed in the above table.

The RANDom Command

The **RANDom** command and the **BINOmial** subcommand were used in Chapter 3 to simulate outcomes from simple random samples where n was the number of trials and p was the probability of success on each trial. We will again use these commands.

Suppose that an opinion poll asks 1785 adults whether they attended a religious service during the past week. Suppose also that 60% of the adult population did not attend. We can use the **RANDom** command to simulate possible outcomes from this survey. The **RANDom** command and the **BINOmial** subcommand generate the number of successes from 1785 independent trials where the answer "No" is considered a success. The values are then divided by 1785 to find $\hat{p}$, the proportion of people that answer "No."

```
MTB > random 100 c1;
SUBC> binomial 1785 .6.
MTB > let c2 = c1/1785
```

We have now generated 100 random samples, each one coming from a binomial distribution with $n = 1785$ and $p = 0.6$. The observations from each of these random samples are the proportions of the 1785 people who said "No." These 100 values are listed and described below.

```
MTB > print c2

C2
   0.601681    0.597759    0.616807    0.587675    0.615126    0.608403
   0.611205    0.594958    0.602241    0.601120    0.592157    0.581513
   0.593277    0.589356    0.606162    0.589916    0.605042    0.578712
   0.592157    0.617367    0.593838    0.591036    0.608403    0.593838
   0.600560    0.616247    0.604482    0.611205    0.611205    0.604482
   0.615126    0.594398    0.595518    0.614566    0.605042    0.599440
   0.589356    0.605042    0.606723    0.592157    0.587675    0.601120
   0.589356    0.597759    0.587675    0.585994    0.603361    0.598880
   0.593277    0.598880    0.588796    0.614566    0.619608    0.611205
   0.620168    0.601120    0.605602    0.591597    0.618487    0.601120
   0.567507    0.600000    0.596639    0.594398    0.601681    0.620728
   0.607843    0.585994    0.590476    0.589356    0.618487    0.607843
   0.582073    0.589356    0.588235    0.607283    0.601120    0.574790
   0.594958    0.598880    0.597759    0.605042    0.597759    0.565826
   0.623529    0.603922    0.593838

MTB > describe c2

                N      MEAN    MEDIAN    TRMEAN     STDEV    SEMEAN
C2            100   0.59970   0.59972   0.59993   0.01164   0.00116

              MIN       MAX        Q1        Q3
C2        0.56583   0.62465   0.59174   0.60714
```

We note that $\hat{p}$, the proportion of people who say "No," varies from about 57% to 63% and that the mean and standard deviation are close to the theoretical values computed as

$$\mu_{\hat{p}} = p = .6$$

$$\sigma_{\hat{p}} = \sqrt{\frac{p(1-p)}{n}} = \sqrt{\frac{.6(1-.6)}{1785}} = .0116$$

Below we examine the shape of the sampling distribution of $\hat{p}$. First we obtain a stemplot and then construct a normal quantile plot to show that the distribution is approximately normal.

```
MTB > stem c2

Stem-and-leaf of C2          N  = 100
Leaf Unit = 0.0010

      2    56 57
      3    57 4
      4    57 8
      7    58 012
     20    58 5577788999999
     37    59 00111222333334444
     50    59 5556777788889
     50    60 00011111111233344
     33    60 5555556677788
     20    61 11112244
     12    61 55667889
      4    62 0034
```

```
MTB > nscores c2 c3
MTB > plot c3 c2


  C3          -                                                          *
              -                                                        *
              -                                                      2
      1.6+                                                         2*
              -                                                  223
              -                                           2  4**
              -                                          4322
              -                                        2*32
      0.0+                                            446
              -                                     55*4
              -                                   62
              -                                  63
              -                            2  4
     -1.6+                             *2
              -                    *    *
              -            *
              -         *
              --+---------+---------+---------+---------+---------+----C2
            0.564     0.576     0.588     0.600     0.612     0.624
```

When the normal approximation to the binomial applies ($np \geq 10$ and $n(1-p) \geq 10$), the **CDF** command can be used to approximate binomial probabilities. The command calculates the probability that an observation is less than or equal to each value in E. The command format is as follows:

```
CDF for values in E [store results in E]
```

Below, we approximate $P(\hat{p} > 0.58)$. We specify the mean and standard deviation of the normal distribution using $\mu_{\hat{p}} = 0.6$ and $\sigma_{\hat{p}} = 0.0116$. The **CDF** command calculates the probability that an observation is less than or equal to a value, so we then subtract the result from 1.

```
MTB > cdf .58;
SUBC> normal .6 .0116.
    0.5800    0.0423
MTB > let k1=1-.0423
MTB > print k1
K1        0.957700
```

Therefore, $P(\hat{p} > 0.58)$ is approximated to be 0.9577.

The **RMEAn** Command

The **RMEAn** command is the rowwise version of the command **MEAN**. It calculates the mean of the numbers in each row and has the following format:

```
RMEAn E,...,E put mean of each row into C
```

Missing observations are omitted from the calculations. The **RMEAn** command can be used to illustrate the central limit theorem. Below we consider a distribution that is not normally distributed. In fact, it is skewed to the right.

```
MTB > info

COLUMN     NAME        COUNT
C1         value           5
C2         prob            5

CONSTANTS USED: NONE

MTB > print c1 c2

  ROW    value      prob

    1        1    0.3487
    2        2    0.3874
    3        3    0.1937
    4        4    0.0574
    5        5    0.0128
```

Below we simulate 1000 observations from this distribution in each of the columns C4 through C14 and then examine the shape of the distribution of C4. As expected, we note that it is skewed to the right.

```
MTB > random 1000 c4-c14;
SUBC> disc c1 c2.
MTB > hist c4

Histogram of C4   N = 1000
Each * represents 10 obs.

Midpoint    Count
       1      349  ***********************************
       2      363  ************************************
       3      218  *********************
       4       56  ******
       5       14  **
```

Now we consider the mean from a sample size of 2. Each observation in C15 is a mean of the values in the same row of C4 and C5.

```
MTB > rmean c4 c5 c15
MTB > name c15 'mean2'
MTB > hist 'mean2'

Histogram of mean2    N = 1000
Each * represents 10 obs.

Midpoint    Count
     1.0      123    *************
     1.2        0
     1.4        0
     1.6      257    *************************
     1.8        0
     2.0      302    ******************************
     2.2        0
     2.4        0
     2.6      168    *****************
     2.8        0
     3.0       99    **********
     3.2        0
     3.4        0
     3.6       39    ****
     3.8        0
     4.0       12    **
```

Notice that the shape of the distribution of $\bar{x}$ (with sample size of 2) is also skewed, but less so compared to the distribution above. Below we consider the distribution of $\bar{x}$ with a sample size of 6 (columns C4 through C9). Notice that it looks more symmetric than the previous distributions.

```
MTB > rmean c4-c9 c16
MTB > name c16 'mean6'
MTB > hist 'mean6'

Histogram of mean6    N = 1000
Each * represents 5 obs.

Midpoint    Count
     1.0        3    *
     1.2       18    ****
     1.4       32    *******
     1.6      224    *********************************************
     1.8      152    *******************************
     2.0      179    ************************************
     2.2      164    *********************************
     2.4      101    *********************
     2.6       93    *******************
     2.8       19    ****
     3.0       14    ***
     3.2        1    *
```

Finally, we consider the sampling distribution of $\bar{x}$ for a sample size of 11 (columns C4 through C14). The distribution below appears to be normal, and the normal quantile plot confirms this.

```
MTB > rmean c4-c14 c17
MTB > name c17 'mean11'
MTB > hist 'mean11'

Histogram of mean11   N = 1000
Each * represents 10 obs.

Midpoint    Count
    1.0        1   *
    1.2        6   *
    1.4       22   ***
    1.6      104   **********
    1.8      204   ********************
    2.0      344   **********************************
    2.2      175   *****************
    2.4       98   *********
    2.6       39   ****
    2.8        6   *
    3.0        1   *

MTB > nscores c17 c18
MTB > plot c18 c17
```

```
  C18    -                                                          *
         -                                                    2
         -                                              4
  2.0+                                            +  +
         -                                    +
         -                                +
         -                          +  +
         -                      +
  0.0+                      +
         -              +  +
         -          +
         -        +
         -      +
         -    +
 -2.0+        +
         -      4  5
         -    2
         -  *
         --+---------+---------+---------+---------+---------+---------+----mean11
         1.05      1.40      1.75      2.10      2.45      2.80
```

Below we compute the mean μ and the standard deviation σ for the distribution specified in C1 and C2.

```
MTB > let k1 = sum(c1*c2)
MTB > print k1
K1       1.99820
MTB > let k2 = sum(c2*(c1-k1)**2)
MTB > print k2
K2       0.887197
MTB > sqrt k2 k3
     ANSWER =        0.9419
```

Therefore, X has mean $\mu = 1.99820$ and standard deviation $\sigma = 0.9419$. Using these values, we obtain the mean and standard deviation for $\bar{x}$, the sample mean with sample size $n = 11$.

$$\mu_{\bar{x}} = \mu = 1.9982$$

$$\sigma_{\bar{x}} = \frac{\sigma}{\sqrt{n}} = \frac{.9419}{\sqrt{11}} = .284$$

These values can now be compared to the mean and standard deviation of the simulated values of $\bar{x}$, given below. Note that the values are very close to the theoretical values obtained above.

```
MTB > describe 'mean11'.

                N      MEAN    MEDIAN    TRMEAN     STDEV    SEMEAN
mean11        1000    1.9995    2.0000    1.9968    0.2861    0.0090

               MIN       MAX        Q1        Q3
mean11      1.0909    2.9091    1.8182    2.1818
```

The `ICHArt` Command

Control charts for individual observations can be produced using the Minitab command **ICHArt**. The format for the command is as follows:

```
ICHArt  for C,...,C
```

A separate control chart is printed for each column specified. In addition to the observations plotted in the control chart, a center line, an upper control limit (UCL) at 3 standard deviations above the center line, and a lower control limit (LCL) at 3 standard deviations below the center line are drawn on the chart. The observations are assumed to have come from a normal distribution with mean μ and standard deviation σ. If μ and σ are not specified, they are estimated from the data.

Professor Moore, who lives a few miles outside a college town, keeps a record of his commuting time. The data (in minutes) are listed in *I.P.S.* in Table 5.3 (page 420) and are stored below in a Minitab worksheet, MOORE.MTW. These individual observations can be recorded on a control chart as illustrated below.

```
MTB > info

   COLUMN     NAME        COUNT
   C1         time          42

CONSTANTS USED: NONE

MTB > ichart c1
```

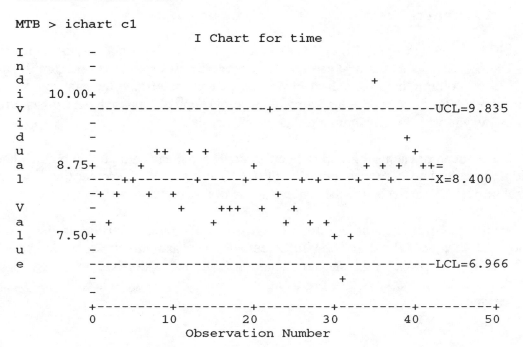

```
                    I Chart for time
I       -
n       -
d       -                                           +
i   10.00+
v       -----------------------+-------------------UCL=9.835
i       -
d       -                                       +
u       -         ++  + +                          +
a    8.75+    +                +          + + +  ++=
l       ----++-------+-----+------+-+----+---+-----X=8.400
        -+ +   + +                 +
V       -          +    +++   +    +
a       - +           +        +  + +
l    7.50+                          + +
u       -
e       -------------------------------------------LCL=6.966
        -                               +

        +---------+---------+---------+---------+---------+
        0        10        20        30        40        50
                    Observation Number
```

Alternatively, the parameters (μ and σ) may be specified with the following subcommands.

```
MU     = K
SIGMa  = K
```

The value of μ is then used for the center line and σ is used in the calculations for the LCL and UCL. The default is that the upper and lower control limits (UCL and LCL) are 3σ above and below μ. The subcommand **SLIMits** can be used to override the 3σ default and specify how many σ limits to use for LCL and UCL. The subcommand format is

```
SLIMits  are K,...,K
```

For example, SLIMits 1 2 plots five lines: a center line, a line at 2σ above the center line, a line at 1σ above, a line at 1σ below the center line, and a line at 2σ below. The default lines, at 3σ limits, are not plotted.

The XBARchart Command

The **XBARchart** command displays a separate $\bar{x}$ chart (a chart of sample means) for each variable specified by the following format.

```
XBARchart  for C,...,C, subgroups are in E
```

E specifies the subgroups (also called samples). If E is a constant, say 5, then Minitab takes the first 5 rows as the first sample, the second 5 rows as the second sample, and so on. If E is a column, then the subscripts in that column determine the subgroups. A new subgroup is formed every time the value in the subgroup column changes (this is different from the way most Minitab commands handle subscripts).

The mean of each subgroup is calculated. These means are plotted on the chart. In addition, a center line, an upper control limit (UCL) at 3σ above the center line, and a lower control limit (LCL) at 3σ below the center line are drawn on the chart.

For example, a manufacturer of high-resolution video terminals measures the tension of fine wires behind the viewing screen. Four measurements are made every hour. The following data contain the measurements for 20 hours. The first four observations are from the first hour, the next four are from the second hour, etc. There are a total of 80 observations.

```
MTB > print c1

sample
   254.1   299.7   206.2   202.6   183.3   224.8   284.0   262.7   276.3
   274.3   243.4   245.8   262.3   309.2   227.7   253.6   228.7   254.6
   236.3   301.5   298.6   278.2   280.6   271.0   290.9   313.8   306.4
   244.2   286.2   287.6   240.1   320.0   179.2   317.6   290.8   245.5
   271.4   225.7   289.3   273.7   299.4   309.2   320.4   343.7   251.7
   296.0   262.5   343.0   188.2   258.1   265.2   302.2   260.2   282.9
   303.6   253.9   267.7   278.3   194.3   316.8   272.5   308.5   265.2
   222.2   304.3   311.3   231.6   332.6   357.4   245.6   225.4   301.7
   236.3   217.5   319.1   331.0   339.5   292.0   259.8   244.7
```

In the following $\bar{x}$ control chart, the mean and standard deviation are estimated from the data.

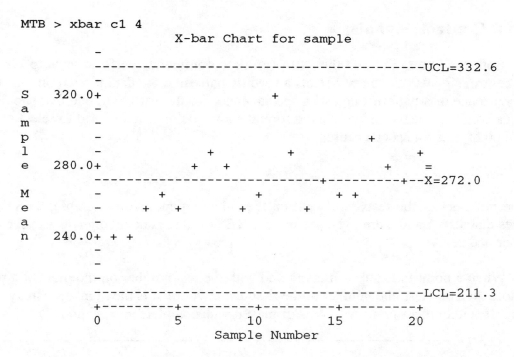

```
MTB > xbar c1 4
                    X-bar Chart for sample
            -
            --------------------------------------------UCL=332.6
            -
 S   320.0+                          +
 a          -
 m          -
 p          -                                +
 l          -           +         +                  +
 e   280.0+       +   +                        +     =
            -------------------------------+---------+--X=272.0
 M          -       +           +           + +
 e          -     + +         +           +
 a          -
 n   240.0+ + +
            -
            -
            -
            --------------------------------------------LCL=211.3
            +---------+---------+---------+---------+
            0         5        10        15        20
                         Sample Number
```

As with the control chart of individual observations (**ICHArt**), it is also possible to specify μ and σ with the **MU** and **SIGMa** subcommands for an $\bar{x}$ control chart. Below we specify the mean and standard deviation for the process, and Minitab computes the mean and standard deviation for $\bar{x}$. These values are $\mu = 275$ and $\sigma = 43$ based on what is known about the process. Minitab uses $\mu_{\bar{x}}$ and $\sigma_{\bar{x}}$ to compute the upper and lower control limits in an $\bar{x}$ control chart. The subcommand **SLIMits** can also be used with the **XBARchart** command.

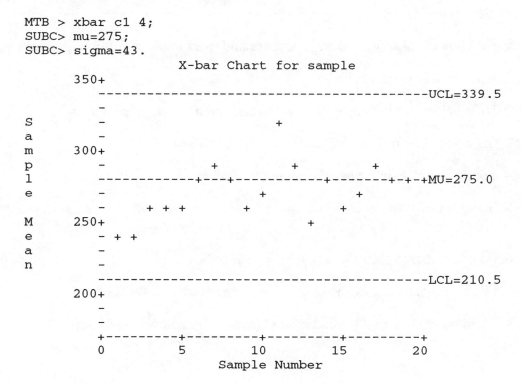

```
MTB > xbar c1 4;
SUBC> mu=275;
SUBC> sigma=43.
                    X-bar Chart for sample
        350+
            --------------------------------------------UCL=339.5
            -
 S          -                    +
 a          -
 m   300+
 p          -           +         +         +
 l          -----------+---+-----------+-------+-+-+MU=275.0
 e          -                  +           +
            -       + + +       +           +
 M   250+                              +
 e          - + +
 a          -
 n          -
            --------------------------------------------LCL=210.5
        200+
            -
            -
            -
            +---------+---------+---------+---------+
            0         5        10        15        20
                         Sample Number
```

Out of Control Signals

Both the `ICHArt` and the `XBARchart` commands perform tests to identify out of control signals. Each test detects a specific pattern in the data plotted on the chart. The occurrence of a pattern suggests a special cause for the variation, one that should be investigated. The `TEST` subcommand format shown below can be used to select one or more of eight tests for special causes.

        TEST   K,...,K

List the numbers of the tests you want on the subcommand. For example, TEST 1 3, specifies that tests 1 and 3 are to be performed. TEST 1:8 says do all eight tests. The tests are described below.

When a point fails a test, it is marked with the test number on the plot. If a point fails more than one test, the number of the first test in your list is the number displayed on the plot. In addition, a summary table is displayed with complete information.

$$+3\sigma \text{ ———————————————————}$$
Zone A
$$+2\sigma \text{ ———————————————————}$$
Zone B
$$+1\sigma \text{ ———————————————————}$$
Zone C
center line ——————————————————
Zone C
$$-1\sigma \text{ ———————————————————}$$
Zone B
$$-2\sigma \text{ ———————————————————}$$
Zone A
$$-3\sigma \text{ ———————————————————}$$

Based on the above zones, the `TEST` subcommand performs the following tests.

1. One point beyond zone A.

2. Nine points in a row in zone C or beyond (on one side of center line).

3. Six points in a row, all increasing or all decreasing.

4. Fourteen points in a row, alternating up and down.

5. Two out of three points in a row in zone A or beyond (on one side of center line).

6. Four out of five points in a row in zone B or beyond (on one side of center line).

7. Fifteen points in a row in zone C (above and below center line).

8. Eight points in a row beyond zone C (above and below center line).

Below we specify that all eight tests are to be done on the control chart of Professor Moore's commuting times. Note that tests 1, 2, 3, 5, and 6 fail, indicating possible out of control signals.

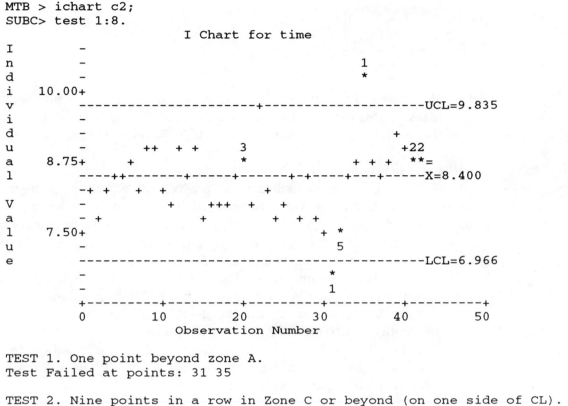

```
MTB > ichart c2;
SUBC> test 1:8.
```

TEST 1. One point beyond zone A.
Test Failed at points: 31 35

TEST 2. Nine points in a row in Zone C or beyond (on one side of CL).
Test Failed at points: 41 42

TEST 3. Six points in a row all increasing or all decreasing.
Test Failed at points: 20

TEST 5. Two of 3 points in a row in zone A or beyond (on one side of CL).
Test Failed at points: 31 32

TEST 6. Four of 5 points in a row in zone B or beyond (on one side of CL).
Test Failed at points: 31 32

EXERCISES

5.4 A factory employs over 3000 workers, of whom 30% are black. If the 15 members of the union executive committee were chosen from the workers without regard to race, the number of blacks on the committee would have the $B(15, 0.3)$ distribution.

(a) Use the **CDF** command with the **BINOmial** subcommand to find the probability that 3 or fewer members of the committee are black.

(b)   We'd like to know the probability that 10 or more members of the committee are white. This is the same as the probability that 5 or fewer members are black. What is this probability?

(c)   The following Minitab commands can be used to simulate the number of blacks on 100 union committees.

```
MTB > RANDOM 100 C1;
SUBC> BINOMIAL 15 .3.
MTB > TABLE C1
```

How many of the simulated committees had 3 or fewer members that were black? How many of the simulated committees had 10 or more members that were white? Compare your results to the answers to (a) and (b).

5.5   A university that is better known for its basketball program than for its academic strength claims that 80% of its basketball players get degrees. An investigation examines the fate of all 20 players who entered the program over a period of several years that ended 5 years ago. Of these players, 10 graduated and the remaining 10 are no longer in school. If the university's claim is true, the number of players who graduate among the 20 studied should have the $B(20, 0.8)$ distribution.

(a)   Use the **PDF** command with the **BINOmial** subcommand to find the probability that exactly 10 players graduate under these assumptions.

(b)   Use the **CDF** command with the **BINOmial** subcommand to find the probability that 10 or fewer players graduate.

(c)   Use the **RANDom** command with the **BINOmial** subcommand to simulate 10 hypothetical basketball teams of size 20. How many of these teams had 10 or fewer players graduate?

5.12   In a test for ESP (extrasensory perception), a subject is told that cards the experimenter can see but he cannot contain either a star, a circle, a wave, or a square. As the experimenter looks at each of 20 cards in turn, the subject names the shape on the card.

(a)   If a subject simply guesses the shape on each card, the probability of a successful guess on a single card is 0.2. Because the cards are independent, the count of successes in 20 cards has a $B(20, 0.2)$ distribution. Use the **CDF** command to find the probability that a subject correctly guesses at least 10 of the 20 shapes. Hint: The probability of guessing at least 10 correctly is the same as the probability of guessing 9 or fewer incorrectly. The distribution of the number of *incorrect* guesses is $B(20, 0.8)$. Why?

(b)   In many repetitions of this experiment with a subject who is guessing, how many cards will the subject guess correctly on the average? Use the **RANDom** command with the **BINOmial** subcommand to simulate the number of correct guesses from 50 repetitions. Use the **MEAN** command to calculate the average number of correct guesses. Is it close to the theoretical mean?

5.15 According to government data, 22% of American children under the age of six live in households with incomes less than the official poverty level. A random sample of 300 children is selected for a study of learning in early childhood.

(a) What is the mean number of children in the sample who come from poverty-level households? What is the standard deviation of this number? Use the **LET** command to calculate these values and store them in K1 and K2.

(b) Use the normal approximation to calculate the probability that at least 80 of the children in the sample live in poverty. This can be done with the following Minitab commands.

```
MTB > cdf 80;
SUBC> norm k1 k2.
```

5.16 One way of checking the effect of undercoverage, nonresponse, and other sources of error in a sample survey is to compare the sample with known demographic facts about the population. About 11% of American adults are black. The number X of blacks in a random sample of 1500 adults should therefore vary with the $B(1500, 0.11)$ distribution.

(a) What are the mean and standard deviation of X?

(b) Use the **CDF** command with the **NORMal** subcommand to find the normal approximation for the probability that the sample will contain 100 or fewer blacks.

5.19 Here is a simple probability model for multiple-choice tests. Suppose that each student has probability p of correctly answering a question chosen at random from a universe of possible questions. (A strong student has a higher p than a weak student.) The correctness of answers to different questions are independent. Julie is a good student for whom $p = 0.75$.

(a) The number of incorrect questions will have a $B(100, .25)$ distribution. Use the **CDF** command with the **BINOmial** subcommand to find the probability that Julie scores 70% or above, that is, the probability that she answers 30 or fewer questions incorrectly.

(b) Use the **LET** command to find the mean and standard deviation of the number of correct questions that Julie will answer on a 100-question test.

(c) Use the **CDF** command and the **NORMal** subcommand to find the normal approximation for the probability that Julie scores 70% or lower on a 100-question test. Comment on the accuracy of the normal approximation.

5.21 An ELISA test was introduced in the mid-1980s to screen donated blood for the presence of antibodies to the AIDS virus. When presented with AIDS-contaminated blood, ELISA gives a positive result (that is, signals that an antibody is present) in about 98% of all cases. Suppose that among the many units of blood that pass through a blood bank in a year there are 20 units containing AIDS antibodies.

(a)   Use the **PDF** command with the **BINOmial** subcommand to find the probability that ELISA will detect all of these cases.

(b)   Use the **CDF** command with the **BINOmial** subcommand to find the probability that more than 2 of the 20 contaminated units will escape detection.

5.28   A bottling company uses a filling machine to fill plastic bottles with a popular cola. The bottles are supposed to contain 300 milliliters (ml). In fact, the contents vary according to a normal distribution with mean $\mu = 298$ ml and standard deviation $\sigma = 3$ ml.

(a)   Use the **CDF** command with the **NORMal** subcommand to find the probability that an individual bottle contains less than 295 ml.

(b)   Use the **LET** command to find the mean and standard deviation for the contents of the bottles in a six-pack. Use the **CDF** command to find the probability that the mean contents of the bottles in a six-pack is less than 295 ml.

5.30   A laboratory weighs filters from a coal mine to measure the amount of dust in the mine atmosphere. Repeated measurements of the weight of dust on the same filter vary normally with standard deviation $\sigma = 0.08$ mg because the weighing is not perfectly precise. The dust on a particular filter actually weighs 123 mg. Repeated weighings will then have the $N(123, 0.08)$ distribution.

(a)   The laboratory reports the mean of 3 weighings. Use the following commands to simulate 100 times the mean of 3 weighings.

```
MTB > RANDOM 100 C1-C3;
SUBC> NORM 123 .08.
MTB > RMEAN C1-C3 put into C4
```

(b)   Describe the simulation results found in C4 using graphical and numerical measures.

5.34   An experiment to compare the nutritive value of normal corn and high-lysine corn divides 40 chicks at random into two groups of 20. One group is fed a diet based on normal corn while the other receives high-lysine corn. At the end of the experiment, inference about which diet is superior is based on the difference $\bar{y} - \bar{x}$ between the mean weight gain $\bar{y}$ of the 20 chicks in the high-lysine group and the mean weight gain $\bar{x}$ of the 20 in the normal corn group. Because of the randomization, the two sample means are independent.

(a)   Suppose that $\mu_x = 360$ grams (g) and $\sigma_x = 55$ g in the population of all chicks fed normal corn, and that $\mu_y = 385$ g and $\sigma_y = 50$ g in the high-lysine population. Use the **LET** command to find the mean and standard deviation of $\bar{x}$ and $\bar{y}$.

(b)   The weight gains are normally distributed in both populations. Simulate the weights of 20 chicks on normal corn and 20 chicks on high-lysine corn. Calculate $\bar{x}$, $\bar{y}$, and $\bar{y} - \bar{x}$.

(c)   What is the distribution of $\bar{y} - \bar{x}$? Simulate the results of the experiment 100 times. How many times does the mean weight gain in the high-lysine group exceed the mean weight gain in the normal group by 25 g or more?

5.39   Leona and Fred are friendly competitors in high school. Both are about to take the ACT college entrance examination. They agree that if one of them scores 5 or more points better than the other, the loser will buy the winner a meal. Suppose that in fact Fred and Leona have equal ability, so that each score varies normally with mean 24 and standard deviation 2. (The variation is due to luck in guessing and the accident of the specific questions being familiar to the student.) The two scores are independent.

(a)   Simulate the results of Leona (in C1) and Fred (in C2) on 100 tries of the ACT test. **LET** C3 be the difference between Fred and Leona's scores. How often do the scores differ by 5 or more points in either direction?

(b)   Use the **DESCribe** command to find the mean and standard deviation for the difference between Fred and Leona's scores.

5.50   The diameter of a bearing deflector in an electric motor is supposed to be 2.205 cm. Experience shows that when the manufacturing process is properly adjusted, it produces items with mean 2.2050 cm and standard deviation 0.0010 cm. A sample of 5 consecutive items is measured once each hour. The sample means $\bar{x}$ for the past 12 hours are given below and in DIAMETER.MTW.

Hour	1	2	3	4	5	6
$\bar{x}$	2.2047	2.2047	2.2050	2.2049	2.2053	2.2043
Hour	7	8	9	10	11	12
$\bar{x}$	2.2036	2.2042	2.2038	2.2045	2.2026	2.2040

Make an **XBARchart** for the deflector diameter, using the **MU** and **SIGMa** subcommands.

```
MTB > set c3
DATA> (5)2.2047 (5)2.2047 (5)2.2050 (5)2.2049 (5)2.2053 (5)2.2043
DATA> (5)2.2036 (5)2.2042 (5)2.2038 (5)2.2045 (5)2.2026 (5)2.2040
DATA> end
```

Also, use the **TEST** subcommand to check both the "one point out" and "run of nine" signals to assess the control of the process. At what point should action have been taken to correct the process as the hourly point was added to the chart?

5.51   Ceramic insulators are baked in lots in a large oven. After the baking, 3 insulators are selected at random from each lot and tested for breaking strength. The mean breaking strength for these samples is plotted on a control chart. The specifications call for a mean breaking strength of at least 10 pounds per square inch (psi). Past experience suggests that if the ceramic is properly formed and baked the standard deviation in the breaking strength is about 1.2 psi. CERAMIC.MTW and the table below provide the sample means from the last 15 lots.

Lot	1	2	3	4	5	6	7	8
$\bar{x}$	12.94	11.45	11.78	13.11	12.69	11.77	11.66	12.60

Lot	9	10	11	12	13	14	15
$\bar{x}$	11.23	12.02	10.93	12.38	7.59	13.17	12.14

Make an **XBARchart** using the **MU** and **SIGMa** subcommands. In this case, a process mean breaking strength greater than 10 psi is acceptable, so points out of control in the high direction do not call for remedial action. With this in mind, use both the "one point out" and "run of nine" signals to assess the control of the process and recommend action. The data can be entered in the required format by using the repeat shorthand with the set command as follows.

```
MTB > set c3
DATA> 3(12.94) 3(11.45) 3(11.78) 3(13.11) 3(12.69)
DATA> 3(11.77) 3(11.66) 3(12.60) 3(11.23) 3(12.02)
DATA> 3(10.93) 3(12.28) 3(7.59) 3(13.17) 3(12.14)
DATA> end
```

5.56   Joe has recorded his weight, measured at the gym after a workout, for several years. The mean is 162 pounds and the standard deviation 1.5 pounds, with no signs of lack of control. An injury keeps Joe away from the gym for several months. The data below give his weight, measured once each week for the first 16 weeks after he returns from the injury. The data are also stored in JOE.MTW.

Week	1	2	3	4	5	6	7	8
Weight	168.7	167.6	165.8	167.5	165.3	163.4	163.0	165.5

Week	9	10	11	12	13	14	15	16
Weight	162.6	160.8	162.3	162.7	160.9	161.3	162.1	161.0

The short-term variation in Joe's weight, estimated from these measurements by advanced methods, is about $\sigma = 1.3$ pounds. Joe has a target of $\mu = 162$ pounds for his weight. Make an **ICHArt** for his measurements, using the **SLIMits** subcommand to mark control limits at $\mu \pm 2\sigma$. Comment on individual points out of control and on runs. Is Joe's weight stable or does it change systematically over this period?

5.57   Professor Moore, who lives a few miles outside a college town, keeps a record of his commuting time. The data (in minutes) appear in Table 5.3 (page 420) of *I.P.S.* and in MOORE.MTW. They cover most of the fall semester, although on some dates the professor was out of town or forgot to set his stopwatch. He also noted unusual occurrences on his record sheet: on October 27, a truck backing into a loading dock delayed him, and on December 5, ice on the windshield forced him to stop and clear the glass.

(a)   Make an **ICHArt** using the **SLIMits** subcommand to include a center line and the control limits $\bar{x} \pm 2s$ on your chart.

(b)   Comment on the control of the process. Is there any indication of an upward or downward trend in driving time? Use the **TEST** subcommand to check whether October 27 and December 5 are identified as potential out of control points.

5.58 A manufacturer of compact disc players uses statistical process control to monitor the quality of the circuit board that contains most of the player's electronic components. Every circuit board is tested for proper function by a computer-directed test bed after assembly. The plant produces 400 circuit boards per shift and the proportion $\hat{p}$ of the 400 boards that fail the test is recorded each day. Company standards call for a failure rate of no more than 10%, or $p = 0.1$.

Day	1	2	3	4	5	6	7	8
$\hat{p}$	.1150	.1600	.1300	.1225	.1000	.1225	.1900	.1150
Day	9	10	11	12	13	14	15	16
$\hat{p}$	.1000	.1600	.1675	.1225	.1375	.1975	.1525	.1675

The **PCHArt** command can be used to make a control chart for proportion defective. The **TEST** and **SLIMits** subcommands can be used with the **PCHArt** command. CIRCUIT.MTW has stored the number defective for each of the 16 days.

(a) Use the following Minitab command to produce a $\hat{p}$ control chart.

```
MTB > PCHART C1 400
```

(b) Use the **TEST** subcommand to check whether points are out of control.

5.73 In an experiment on learning foreign languages, researchers studied the effect of delaying oral practice when beginning language study. The researchers randomly assigned 23 beginning students of Russian to an experimental group and another 23 to a control group. The control group began speaking practice immediately while the experimental group delayed speaking for 4 weeks. At the end of the semester both groups took a standard test of comprehension of spoken Russian. Suppose that in the population of all beginning students, the test scores under the control method vary according to the $N(32, 6)$ distribution. The population distribution when oral practice is delayed is $N(29, 5)$.

(a) What is the sampling distribution of the mean score $\bar{x}$ in the control group in many repetitions of the experiment? Use the **LET** command to find the mean and standard deviation for $\bar{x}$ (the mean in the control group) and $\bar{y}$ (the mean in the experimental group).

(b) Use the **RANDom** command to simulate the results of this experiment 50 times, with the $\bar{x}$ observations stored in C1 and the $\bar{y}$ observations in C2. **LET** C3 be the difference $\bar{x} - \bar{y}$ between the mean scores in the two groups. Examine the data in C3 and comment on the distribution of $\bar{x} - \bar{y}$.

(c) Estimate the probability that the experiment will find (misleadingly) that the experimental group has a mean at least as large as that of the control group by finding the proportion of values in C3 that are positive.

5.74   We can observe the distribution of a statistic in repeated sampling by simulation. Consider a large population of young women whose heights vary according to the normal distribution with mean $\mu = 65.5$ inches and standard deviation $\sigma = 2.5$ inches. Use the RANDom command with the NORMal subcommand to draw repeated SRSs of size $n = 9$ from this population and observe the behavior of the sample mean $\bar{x}$ in repeated sampling. The sampling distribution of $\bar{x}$ is the theoretical distribution that would result from an indefinitely large number of samples; the distribution we observe in this exercise is an approximation based on a few samples.

(a)   You can simulate an SRS of size 9 by generating 9 observations from the $N(65.5, 2.5)$ distribution. Do this 100 times and save the 100 SRSs that result.

(b)   Now calculate the sample mean $\bar{x}$ for each sample and save the 100 values of $\bar{x}$.

(c)   Investigate the distribution of the 100 values of $\bar{x}$. What are the mean and standard deviation of these data?

Chapter 6
Introduction to Inference

Commands to be covered in this chapter:

```
ZINTerval [K% confidence] sigma=K, for  C,...,C
ZTESt [of mu = K] assumed sigma = K on C,...,C
INVCdf for values in E [ store results in E]
```

The ZINTerval Command

The **ZINTerval** command calculates a normal theory confidence interval for the mean, with σ known, separately on each column. The command format follows.

```
ZINTerval [K% confidence] sigma=K, for  C,...,C
```

This interval goes from $\bar{x} - z^*\left(\sigma/\sqrt{n}\right)$ to $\bar{x} + z^*\left(\sigma/\sqrt{n}\right)$, where $\bar{x}$ is the mean of the data, n is the sample size, and z^* is the value from the normal table corresponding to K percent confidence. If K is not specified, K = 95 is used. For example,

```
MTB > zinterval 90 .3  C1
```

If the value of K for the confidence level is less than 1, it is assumed to be a confidence coefficient and not a percentage, and is multiplied by 100. That is, if you use the command

```
MTB >  zint .80 1.2 C1
```

an 80% confidence interval is calculated.

Consider a laboratory that analyzes specimens of a pharmaceutical product to determine the concentration of the active ingredient. The results of 40 repeated measurements are given below and in ACTIVE.MTW.

```
MTB > print c1

concent
    0.8370    0.8460    0.8351    0.8464    0.8452    0.8362    0.8424    0.8468
    0.8279    0.8275    0.8401    0.8338    0.8387    0.8395    0.8278    0.8408
    0.8532    0.8393    0.8390    0.8421    0.8296    0.8230    0.8449    0.8293
    0.8407    0.8478    0.8366    0.8524    0.8362    0.8472    0.8411    0.8411
    0.8349    0.8426    0.8407    0.8409    0.8516    0.8511    0.8291    0.8314
```

These measurements closely follow a normal distribution. The standard deviation of this distribution is known to be $\sigma = 0.0068$. Below, we will use the `ZINTerval` command to compute 90%, 95%, and 99% confidence intervals.

```
MTB > zinterval 90 .0068 c1

THE ASSUMED SIGMA =0.00680

                   N      MEAN    STDEV   SE MEAN    90.0 PERCENT C.I.
concent           40   0.83943  0.00747  0.00108   ( 0.83765, 0.84120)

MTB > zint .0068 c1

THE ASSUMED SIGMA =0.00680

                   N      MEAN    STDEV   SE MEAN    95.0 PERCENT C.I.
concent           40   0.83943  0.00747  0.00108   ( 0.83731, 0.84154)

MTB > zint .99 .0068 'concent'

THE ASSUMED SIGMA =0.00680

                   N      MEAN    STDEV   SE MEAN    99.0 PERCENT C.I.
concent           40   0.83943  0.00747  0.00108   ( 0.83665, 0.84220)
```

Note that we specified a 90% interval by letting K = 90, we specified a 99% interval by letting K = 0.99, and Minitab calculated a 95% confidence interval when we did not specify a value for K. The values for MEAN and STDEV listed with the confidence intervals are the same as those that would be obtained using the `DESCribe` command. The value given for SE MEAN is calculated with the known value of σ as follows.

$$\frac{\sigma}{\sqrt{n}} = \frac{.0068}{\sqrt{40}} = .00108.$$

The `ZTESt` Command

The `ZTESt` command performs a normal theory test with σ known, separately on each column. If K is not specified, $\mu = 0$ is used. The command format is

```
ZTESt [of mu = K] assumed sigma = K on C,...,C
```

If no subcommand is given, a two-sided test is done. Otherwise, a subcommand specifies the alternative hypothesis with the following form.

```
ALTernative = K
```

If ALT = −1, then $\mu < $ K is used. If ALT = 1, $\mu > $ K is used. For example, if we wish to test the hypothesis that $\mu = 0.84$ against the alternative $\mu \neq 0.84$ for the data given above, we do not need to use a subcommand, as illustrated below.

```
MTB > ztest .84 .0068 c1

TEST OF MU = 0.84000 VS MU N.E.  0.84000
THE ASSUMED SIGMA = 0.00680

              N      MEAN    STDEV   SE MEAN        Z    P VALUE
concent      40   0.83987  0.00759  0.00108    -0.12       0.91
```

If instead we wish to test the hypothesis that $\mu = 0.84$ against the alternative $\mu < 0.84$ for the data given above, we use the **ALTernative** subcommand with $K = -1$. This is illustrated below.

```
MTB > ztest .84 .0068 c1;
SUBC> alt -1.

TEST OF MU = 0.84000 VS MU L.T.  0.84000
THE ASSUMED SIGMA = 0.00680

              N      MEAN    STDEV   SE MEAN        Z    P VALUE
concent      40   0.83987  0.00759  0.00108    -0.12       0.45
```

Note that the *P*-value given is smaller for the one-sided test. In fact, it is equal to half the *P*-value computed for the two-sided test. In both tests, the value is too high to reject the null hypothesis.

The **INVCdf** Command

The **INVCdf** command can be used to find the critical value that would be required to reject the null hypothesis at a particular significance level. The **CDF** command, which was introduced in Chapter 1, calculates the area associated with a value. The **INVCdf** command does just the opposite; it calculates a value associated with an area. We can find the value of *z* that has a specific area below it. If no subcommand is specified, then the distribution is assumed to be normal with $\mu = 0$ and $\sigma = 1$. The **INVCdf** command has the following format.

```
INVCdf for values in E [store results in E]
```

Suppose that we wish to use a 1% significance criterion for the example above. Since the test is one-sided, the probability in the tail must be 0.01 or less, so we find the value of *z* that has area 0.01 below it.

```
MTB > invc .01
    0.0100    -2.3263
```

Therefore, we would reject the null hypothesis at the 1% level of significance if

$$z < -2.3263$$

EXERCISES

6.5   You measure the weights of a random sample of 24 male runners. The sample mean is $\bar{x} = 60$ kilograms (kg). Suppose that the standard deviation of the population is known to be $\sigma = 5$ kg.

(a)   Use the **RANDom** command to simulate the weights of 24 male runners with a weight distribution that is $N(60, 5)$. Use the **ZINTerval** command to compute a 95% confidence interval for μ, the mean of the population from which the sample is drawn.

(b)   Repeat the simulation in 39 additional columns. Give 95% confidence intervals for each column. How many of the computed confidence intervals do not include $\mu = 60$?

(c)   Find a 99% confidence interval for the mean weight μ for the weights in the first column. Is the 99% confidence interval wider or narrower than the 95% interval found in (a)?

6.11   Below and in CRANK.MTW are measurements (in millimeters) of a critical dimension on a sample of auto engine crankshafts.

224.120	224.001	224.017	223.982	223.989	223.961
223.960	224.089	223.987	223.976	223.902	223.980
224.098	224.057	223.913	223.999		

The data come from a production process that is known to have standard deviation $\sigma = 0.060$ mm.

(a)   Use the **NSCOres** and **PLOT** commands to make a normal quantile plot to verify that the distribution is very close to normal.

(b)   The process mean is supposed to be $\mu = 224$ mm but can drift away from this target during production. Use the **ZINTerval** command to compute a 95% confidence interval for the process mean at the time these crankshafts were produced.

(c)   Do these data give evidence that the process mean is not equal to the target value 224 mm? Use the **ZTESt** command to find the P-value for the following hypothesis test.

$$H_0: \mu = 224$$
$$H_A: \mu \neq 224$$

6.12   Below and in DRP.MTW are the Degree of Reading Power scores for a sample of 44 third grade students.

40	26	39	14	42	18	25	43	46	27	19
47	19	26	35	34	15	44	40	38	31	46
52	25	35	35	33	29	34	41	49	28	52
47	35	48	22	33	41	51	27	14	54	45

(a) Suppose that the standard deviation of the population of DRP scores is known to be $\sigma = 11$. Examine these data to check that the distribution is close to normal. Give a 99% confidence interval for the population mean score.

(b) These students can be considered to be an SRS of the third graders in a suburban school district. The researcher believes that the mean score μ of all third graders in this district is higher than the national mean, which is 32. Do these data give evidence that the mean is higher than 32? Use the **ZTESt** command with the **ALT** subcommand to test the following hypotheses.

$$H_0: \mu = 32$$
$$H_a: \mu > 32$$

(c) Give the *P*-value, and then interpret the result in plain language.

6.34 A computer has a random number generator designed to produce random numbers that are uniformly distributed in the interval from 0 to 1. If this is true, the numbers generated come from a population with $\mu = 0.5$ and $\sigma = 0.2887$. Simulate 100 numbers using the **RANDom** command with the **UNIForm** subcommand. We want to test

$$H_0: \mu = .5$$
$$H_a: \mu \neq .5$$

(a) Use the **ZTESt** command to find the *P*-value for this test.
(b) Is the result significant at the 5% level ($\alpha = 0.05$)?
(c) Is the result significant at the 1% level ($\alpha = 0.01$)?

6.47 Every user of statistics should understand the distinction between statistical significance and practical importance. A sufficiently large sample will declare very small effects statistically significant. Let us suppose that Scholastic Aptitude Test mathematics (SAT-M) scores in the absence of coaching vary normally with mean $\mu = 475$ and $\sigma = 100$. Suppose further that coaching may change μ but does not change σ. An increase in the SAT-M score from 475 to 478 is of no importance in seeking admission to college, but this unimportant change can be statistically significant. To see this, calculate the *P*-value for the test of

$$H_0: \mu = 475$$
$$H_a: \mu > 475$$

in each of the following situations. The data are found in SATM.MTW.

(a) A coaching service coaches 100 students; their SAT-M scores average $\bar{x} = 478$. Use the **INVCdf** command to find the critical value of $\bar{x}$ for 100 students.

(b) By the next year, the service has coached 1000 students; their SAT-M scores average $\bar{x} = 478$. Use the **INVCdf** command to find the critical value of $\bar{x}$ for 1000 students.

6.63   Patients with chronic kidney failure may be treated by dialysis, using a machine that removes toxic wastes from the blood, a function normally performed by the kidneys. Kidney failure and dialysis can cause other changes, such as retention of phosphorus, that must be corrected by changes in diet. A study of the nutrition of dialysis patients measured the level of phosphorus in the blood of several patients on six occasions. Stored in DIALYSIS.MTW and below are the data for one patient (milligrams of phosphorus per deciliter of blood). The measurements are separated in time and can be considered an SRS of the patient's blood phosphorus level. (Data provided by Joan M. Susic.)

5.6   5.1   4.6   4.8   5.7   6.4

(a)   Assuming that this level varies normally with $\sigma = 0.9$ mg/dl, use the **ZINTerval** command to give a 90% confidence interval for the mean blood phosphorus level.

(b)   The normal range of phosphorus in the blood is considered to be 2.6 to 4.8 mg/dl. Use the **ZTESt** command to determine whether there is strong evidence that the patient has a mean phosphorus level that exceeds 4.8.

6.65   Sulfur compounds cause "off-odors" in wine, so that oenologists (wine experts) have determined the odor threshold, the lowest concentration of a compound that the human nose can detect. For example, the odor threshold for dimethyl sulfide (DMS) is given in the oenology literature as 25 micrograms per liter of wine (μg/l). Untrained noses may be less sensitive, however. Below and in WINE.MTW are the DMS odor thresholds for 10 beginning students of oenology. Assume (this is not realistic) that the standard deviation of the odor threshold for untrained noses is known to be $\sigma = 7$ μg/l.

31   31   43   36   23   34   32   30   20   24

(a)   Make a **STEM-and-leaf** diagram to verify that the distribution is roughly symmetric with no outliers. Use the **NSCOres** and **PLOT** commands to confirm that there are no systematic departures from normality.

(b)   Use the **ZINTerval** command to give a 95% confidence interval for the mean DMS odor threshold among all beginning oenology students.

(c)   Are you convinced that the mean odor threshold for beginning students is higher than the published threshold, 25 μg/l? Use the **ZTESt** command to carry out a significance test to justify your answer.

Chapter 7
Inference for Distributions

Commands to be covered in this chapter:

```
TINTerval [with K percent confidence] for data in C,...,C
TTESt [of mu = K] on data in C,...,C
INVCdf for values in E [store results in E]
STESt [of median = K] for data in C,...,C
TWOSample t [K% confidence] for data in C and C
TWOT [K% confidence] for data in C, subscripts in C
```

The TINTerval Command

The **TINTerval** command calculates a *t*-confidence interval for the mean. The confidence interval is calculated separately for each column specified in the following format.

```
TINTerval [with K percent confidence] for data in C,...,C
```

If the percent confidence is not specified, a 95% confidence interval is calculated. Below, we calculate a 99% confidence interval for Newcomb's measurements of the speed of light with the two outliers deleted. The data are discussed in Examples 1.1 and 7.2 of *I.P.S.* and are given in NEWCOMB.MTW.

```
MTB > let c1(10)= '*'
MTB > let c1(6) = '*'
MTB > print c1

speed
    28    26    33    24    34     *    27    16    40     *    29
    22    24    21    25    30    23    29    31    19    24    20
    36    32    36    28    25    21    28    29    37    25    28
    26    30    32    36    26    30    22    36    23    27    27
    28    27    31    27    26    33    26    32    32    24    39
    28    24    25    32    25    29    27    28    29    16    23

MTB > tinterval 99 c1

               N      MEAN    STDEV   SE MEAN    99.0 PERCENT C.I.
speed         64    27.750    5.083    0.635   ( 26.062,  29.438)
```

129

If we use the **DESCribe** command to calculate the MEAN, STDEV, and SEMEAN, we note that the results are the same as above.

	N	N*	MEAN	MEDIAN	TRMEAN	STDEV	SEMEAN
speed	64	2	27.750	27.500	27.741	5.083	0.635

	MIN	MAX	Q1	Q3
speed	16.000	40.000	24.250	31.000

The **TTESt** Command

The **TTESt** command performs a separate *t* test for each column specified in the following format.

        TTEST [of mu = K] on data in C,...,C

By default, Minitab does a two-sided test with the test mean $\mu = 0$. Other values for μ can be specified. To do one-sided tests, use the **ALTErnative** subcommand. As with the **ZTESt** command, the subcommand format is

        ALTernative = K

If ALT = -1 then $\mu < K$ is used. If ALT = $+1$, $\mu > K$ is used. Below we illustrate the **TTESt** command by testing whether or not Newcomb's measurements are consistent with the speed of light equal to 33.02. We use Minitab to test

$$H_0: \mu = 33.02$$
$$H_a: \mu \neq 33.02$$

To test this, we specify 33.02 for μ in the **TTESt** command.

        MTB > ttest mu = 33.02 c1

        TEST OF MU = 33.020 VS MU N.E. 33.020

	N	MEAN	STDEV	SE MEAN	T	P VALUE
speed	64	27.750	5.083	0.635	-8.29	0.0000

The *P*-value is reported as 0.0000. This means that it is less than 0.0001. We can safely reject H_0.

The **INVCdf** Command

To determine the critical value of *t* that would be required to reject the null hypothesis, we can use the **INVCdf** command with the **T** subcommand. The subcommand format for Student's *t* distribution with K degrees of freedom is

        T with degrees of freedom = K

Since the above test was two-sided, we would reject at the 5% level of significance as long as the probability of being in each tail is less than 2.5%. Below, we use Minitab to find the value of t with area 0.025 below it. We specify that there are 63 degrees of freedom since $n = 64$.

```
MTB > invcdf .025;
SUBC> t 63.
    0.0250   -1.9984
```

Therefore, we would reject H_0 for any value of t that is less than -1.9984. Since the test is two-sided and Student's t distribution is symmetric, we would also reject H_0 for any value of t that is larger than 1.9984.

Matched Pairs

In a matched pairs study, subjects are matched in pairs and the outcomes are compared within each matched pair. For example, in the worksheet below, we have teachers scores on the Modern Language Association's listening test of understanding spoken French both before and after 4 weeks of immersion in French. The pretest scores are from before the 4 weeks of immersion and the posttest scores are for after the 4 weeks of immersion. This example is described in Example 7.3 of *I.P.S.* The data are given in MLA.MTW.

```
MTB > info

COLUMN    NAME      COUNT
C1        teacher     20
C2        pretest     20
C3        posttest    20

CONSTANTS USED: NONE
```

To determine whether the teachers' comprehension improved, we will test

$$H_0 : \mu = 0$$
$$H_a : \mu > 0$$

where we are considering the average test improvement. Below we compute the improvement by subtracting the pretest score from the posttest score. Then the **TTESt** command is used.

```
MTB > let c4 = c3-c2
MTB > name c4 'change'
MTB > ttest c4;
SUBC> alt +1.

TEST OF MU = 0.000 VS MU G.T. 0.000

              N      MEAN     STDEV    SE MEAN       T    P VALUE
change       20     2.500     2.893      0.647    3.86     0.0005
```

The small value given for the *P*-value means that it is unlikely for the observed value of *t* to have occurred by chance alone. We have strong evidence that the immersion in French was effective in raising scores.

A 90% confidence interval for the mean improvement is computed below. Note that the computed interval does not include 0, also giving evidence that the mean is not equal to 0.

```
MTB > tint 90 c4

                  N       MEAN    STDEV  SE MEAN   90.0 PERCENT C.I.
change           20      2.500    2.893    0.647  (   1.381,   3.619)
```

The STESt Command

In the above example, a plot of the data using the   STEM-and-leaf command illustrates that the data are granular and include an outlier.

```
MTB > stem c4

Stem-and-leaf of change    N  = 20
Leaf Unit = 1.0

     1    -0 6
     1    -0
     1    -0
     2    -0 0
     6     0 0011
    (9)    0 222333333
     5     0
     5     0 66666
```

This means that the *P*-value computed from the one-sample *t* test above is only roughly correct.

Alternatively, a sign test does not make any assumptions about the shape of the population. Minitab's **STESt** command will do the calculations for a sign test. The command format is

```
STESt [of median = K] for data in C,...,C
```

The **STESt** command performs a separate sign test of the null hypothesis

$$H_0: \text{median} = K$$

for each column. If K is not specified, $K = 0$ is used. Unless the subcommand **ALTernative** is used, Minitab tests the alternative hypothesis

$$H_a: \text{median} \neq K$$

To do a matched pairs sign test use **STESt** using the differences. For samples of size 50 or less, the exact *P*-value is used. For samples larger than 50, the *P*-value is computed using a normal approximation with continuity correction. The **STESt** command is illustrated below using the differences between the posttest and pretest scores. To determine whether the teachers' comprehension improved, we will test

$$H_0: \text{median} = 0$$

$$H_a: \text{median} > 0$$

where we are considering the median test improvement.

```
MTB > stest c4;
SUBC> alt +1.

SIGN TEST OF MEDIAN = 0.00000 VERSUS  G.T.   0.00000

                 N  BELOW  EQUAL  ABOVE   P-VALUE   MEDIAN
change          20     1      3     16    0.0001    3.000
```

The *P*-value obtained above is small (0.0001), so there is strong evidence that the course improved performance on the listening test.

The **TWOSample t** Command

Two Minitab commands are available to do two-sample *t* procedures. These are the **TWOSample t** command and the **TWOT** command. The commands differ only in the way the input data are arranged. The **TWOSample t** command performs a two (independent) sample *t* test and confidence interval with the data for each sample in separate columns. The command format is give below.

```
TWOSample t [K% confidence] for data in C and C
```

Use **TWOSample t** if your data are in separate columns as in the following example.

Example 7.8 of *I.P.S.* describes an educator who believes that new directed reading activities in the classroom will improve reading ability for elementary school pupils. She arranges for a third grade class of 21 students to follow these activities for an 8-week period. These students are compared to a control classroom of 23 students. At the end of the 8 weeks, all students are given a reading test.   The scores are recorded in a Minitab worksheet, DIRECTED.MTW in two columns, 'treat' and 'control'.

```
MTB > desc c1 c2

              N    MEAN   MEDIAN   TRMEAN   STDEV   SEMEAN
treat        21   51.48    53.00    51.89   11.01     2.40
control      23   41.52    42.00    40.95   17.15     3.58

             MIN     MAX      Q1       Q3
treat      24.00   71.00   43.50    58.50
control    10.00   85.00   28.00    54.00
```

The **TWOSample t** command is used to test

$$H_0: \mu_1 = \mu_2$$

$$H_a: \mu_1 > \mu_2$$

Minitab tests the null hypothesis and calculates a confidence interval for $\mu_1 - \mu_2$. If the percent confidence is not specified, a 95% confidence interval is calculated. The **ALTernative** subcommand is used to do one-sided tests. If ALT −1 is used, then $\mu_1 < \mu_2$ is used for the alternative hypothesis. If ALT 1 is used, then $\mu_1 > \mu_2$ is the alternative hypothesis. If the subcommand is not given, $\mu_1 \neq \mu_2$ is used.

```
MTB > twos c1 c2;
SUBC> alt +1.

TWOSAMPLE T FOR Treat VS Control
            N      MEAN     STDEV    SE MEAN
Treat      21      51.5      11.0      2.4
Control    23      41.5      17.1      3.6

95 PCT CI FOR MU Treat - MU Control: (1.2, 18.7)

TTEST MU Treat = MU Control (VS GT): T= 2.31   P=0.013   DF=  37
```

Since the *P*-value is small (0.013), the data give evidence to support the thesis that directed reading activity improves the test score. Although the confidence interval does not include 0, the margin of error is almost 9 points. The data do not allow a precise estimate of the average improvement.

Unless the **POOLed** subcommand is used, the **TWOSample t** command does not assume that the populations have equal variances, so the test statistic is

$$t = \frac{\overline{X}_1 - \overline{X}_2}{\sqrt{\dfrac{s_1^2}{n_1} + \dfrac{s_2^2}{n_2}}}$$

This statistic has approximately a *t* distribution with degrees of freedom given by:

$$df = \frac{\dfrac{s_1^2}{n_1} + \dfrac{s_2^2}{n_2}}{\dfrac{1}{n_1 - 1}\left(\dfrac{s_1^2}{n_1}\right)^2 + \dfrac{1}{n_2 - 1}\left(\dfrac{s_2^2}{n_2}\right)^2}$$

Minitab truncates the number to an integer, if necessary.

If the **POOLed** subcommand is used, Minitab uses a pooled procedure, which assumes the two populations have equal variances. The pooled variance is estimated to be

$$s_p^2 = \frac{(n_1 - 1)s_1^2 + (n_2 - 1)s_2^2}{n_1 + n_2 - 2}$$

and the test statistic is

$$t = \frac{\overline{X}_1 - \overline{X}_2}{s_p \sqrt{\dfrac{1}{n_1} + \dfrac{1}{n_2}}}$$

This statistic has a t distribution with $n_1 + n_2 - 2$ degrees of freedom. The pooled procedure is slightly more powerful than the method that does not assume the variances are equal, and can be seriously in error if the variances are not equal. Thus, the POOLed subcommand should not be used unless the variances are known to be equal.

The TWOT Command

The TWOT command also performs a two (independent) sample t test and confidence interval. This command is used when the data for both samples are in the first column. The second column contains sample subscripts. The command format follows.

```
TWOT [K percent confidence] for data in C, subscripts in C
```

In the previous example, it would be appropriate to use the TWOT command if the data were stored so that all test scores were in one column and the group (1 or 2) was stored in a second column as illustrated below. The DESCribe command is used with the BY subcommand to summarize the data and then the TWOT command is used to obtain the same results as above.

The data are often entered in the format required by the TWOT command. However, our data were entered in individual columns, so we demonstrate the command after using the STACk command to arrange the data used above into the required format. We also need a column to identify which group each data point belongs to. The SUBScripts subcommand in STACk will provide these codes automatically.

```
MTB > stack c1 c2 c3;
SUBC> subs c4.
MTB > name c3 'score' c4 'group'
MTB > print c3 c4

 ROW   score   group

   1      24       1
   2      33       1
   3      43       1
   4      43       1
   5      43       1
   .       .       .
   .       .       .
   .       .       .
  42      62       2
  43      60       2
  44      85       2
```

```
MTB > desc c3;
SUBC> by c4.
```

	group	N	MEAN	MEDIAN	TRMEAN	STDEV	SEMEAN
score	1	21	51.48	53.00	51.89	11.01	2.40
	2	23	41.52	42.00	40.95	17.15	3.58

	group	MIN	MAX	Q1	Q3
score	1	24.00	71.00	43.50	58.50
	2	10.00	85.00	28.00	54.00

```
MTB > twot c3 c4;
SUBC> alt +1.

TWOSAMPLE T FOR score
group   N      MEAN      STDEV    SE MEAN
1       21     51.5      11.0      2.4
2       23     41.5      17.1      3.6

95 PCT CI FOR MU 1 - MU 2: (1.2, 18.7)

TTEST MU 1 = MU 2 (VS GT): T= 2.31  P=0.013  DF=  37
```

The **ALTErnative** subcommand was used to do one-sided tests. Since the **POOLed** subcommand was not used, **TWOT** did not assume that the populations have equal variance.

The *F* Test for Equality of Variance*

We will illustrate an *F* test on data coming from a medical experiment comparing the effects of calcium and a placebo on the blood pressure of black men. The data are given in SYSTOLIC.MTW and in the description of Exercise 7.46. That exercise considers using pooled two-sample *t* procedures. Because these procedures require equal population standard deviations, we will test

$$H_0: \sigma_1 = \sigma_2$$
$$H_a: \sigma_1 \neq \sigma_2$$

The hypothesis of equal spread can be tested in Minitab using an *F* test. Before computing the *F* statistic, it is important to check that the distributions being considered are normal. The *F* test is not recommended for distributions that are not normal. Before we calculate the *F* statistic, it is important to verify that the distributions are normal. This is done using the **NSCOres** and **PLOT** commands. Boxplots are also useful for visually checking whether the variances appear to be different.

The *F* statistic is the ratio of the sample variances,

$$F = \frac{s_1^2}{s_2^2}$$

---

* This section can be omitted without loss of continuity.

with the larger sample variance in the numerator. The test statistic can be computed with Minitab using the **LET** command as illustrated below.

```
MTB > desc c3 c6

                      N      MEAN    MEDIAN    TRMEAN    STDEV    SEMEAN
        Calcium      10      5.00      4.00      4.62     8.74      2.76
        Placebo      11     -0.64     -1.00     -0.89     5.87      1.77

                    MIN       MAX        Q1        Q3
        Calcium   -5.00     18.00     -3.25     12.50
        Placebo  -11.00     12.00     -3.00      3.00

MTB > let k1=std('calcium')/std('placebo')
MTB > let k1 = k1**2
MTB > print k1
K1        2.21870
```

Once the F statistic has been calculated, the **CDF** command with the **F** subcommand can be used to find the P-value of the observations. The subcommand format is

```
F with df numerator = K, df denominator = K
```

Below, we use the **CDF** command with the **F** subcommand to find $P(F < 2.2187)$.

```
MTB > cdf k1;
SUBC> f 9 10.
    2.2187    0.8848
```

Since the test is two-sided, the P-value is equal to $2 \times P(F < 2.2187)$. In the example above, the P-value is $2 \times (1 - 0.8848) = 0.23$. Therefore, the difference between the spread on the two tests is not statistically significant. However, since one of the populations shows some departure from normality, we can't be fully sure of the conclusion.

The **INVCdf** command can be used with the **F** subcommand to find the critical value of F that would be required to reject the null hypothesis at the 5% significance level. Since the test is two-sided, the probability in each tail must be 0.025 or less, so we find the the value of F that has probability 0.975 of being less.

```
MTB > invcdf .975;
SUBC> f 9 10.
    0.9750    3.7790
```

Therefore, for the sample sizes shown above, the F statistic would have to be at least 3.779 to reject H_0 at the 5% level.

EXERCISES

7.14   Stored in CRANK.MTW and given below are measurements (in millimeters) of a critical dimension for 16 auto engine crankshafts.

224.120	224.001	224.017	223.982	223.989	223.961
223.960	224.089	223.987	223.976	223.902	223.980
224.098	224.057	223.913	223.999		

The mean dimension is supposed to be 224 mm and the variability of the manufacturing process is unknown. Is there evidence that the mean dimension is not 224 mm?

(a)   Check the data graphically for outliers or strong skewness that might threaten the validity of the *t* procedures.

(b)   Do these data give evidence that the process mean is not equal to the target value 224 mm? Use the **TTESt** command to find the exact *P*-value for the following hypothesis test.

$$H_0: \mu = 224$$
$$H_a: \mu \neq 224$$

What do you conclude?

7.15   How accurate are radon detectors of a type sold to homeowners? To answer this question, university researchers placed 12 detectors in a chamber that exposed them to 105 picocuries per liter (pCi/l) of radon. The detector readings are given below and in RADON.MTW. (Data provided by Diana Schellenberg, Purdue University School of Health Sciences.)

91.9	97.8	111.4	122.3	105.4	95.0
103.8	99.6	96.6	119.3	104.8	101.7

(a)   Make a **STEM-and-leaf** diagram of the data to determine whether the distribution is skewed strongly enough to forbid use of the *t* procedures.

(b)   Is there convincing evidence that the mean reading of all detectors of this type differs from the true value 105? Use the **TTESt** command, then write a brief conclusion.

7.18   The design of controls and instruments has a large effect on how easily people can use them. A student project investigated this effect by asking 25 right-handed students to turn a knob (with their right hands) that moved an indicator by screw action. There were two identical instruments, one with a right-hand thread (the knob turns clockwise) and the other with a left-hand thread (the knob must be turned counterclockwise). The table below and HAND.MTW give the times required (in seconds) to move the indicator a fixed distance. (Data provided by Timothy Sturm.)

Subject	Right thread	Left thread	Subject	Right thread	Left thread
1	113	137	14	107	87
2	105	105	15	118	166
3	130	133	16	103	146
4	101	108	17	111	123
5	138	115	18	104	135
6	118	170	19	111	112
7	87	103	20	89	93
8	116	145	21	78	76
9	75	78	22	100	116
10	96	107	23	89	78
11	122	84	24	85	101
12	103	148	25	88	123
13	116	147			

(a)   The project hoped to show that right-handed people find right-hand threads easier to use. Use the **TTESt** command to test the appropriate H_0 and H_a about the mean time required to complete the task.

(b)   Give the *P*-value and report your conclusions.

(c)   Use the **TINTerval** command to give a 90% confidence interval for the mean time advantage of right-hand over left-hand threads in the setting of the previous exercise. Do you think that the time saved would be of practical importance if the task were performed many times, for example by an assembly line worker? To help answer this question, find the mean time for right-hand threads as a percent of the mean time for left-hand threads.

(ed   Use the **STESt** command to assess whether right-handed people find right-hand threads easier to use. Are your conclusions different from part (b)?

7.20   The table below and MLA.MTW give the pretest and posttest scores on the MLA listening test in Spanish for 20 high school Spanish teachers who attended an intensive summer course in Spanish. The setting is identical to the French institute described in Example 7.3. (Data provided by Joseph A. Wipf, Foreign Languages and Literatures, Purdue University.)

Subject	Pretest	Posttest	Subject	Pretest	Posttest
1	30	29	11	30	32
2	28	30	12	29	28
3	31	32	13	31	34
4	26	30	14	29	32
5	20	16	15	34	32
6	30	25	16	20	27
7	34	31	17	26	28
8	15	18	18	25	29
9	28	33	19	31	32
10	20	25	20	29	32

(a)   We hope to show that attending the institute improves listening skills. State an appropriate H_0 and H_a. Be sure to identify the parameters appearing in the hypotheses.

(b)   Make a graphical check for outliers or strong skewness in the data that you will use in your statistical test, and report your conclusions on the validity of the test.

(c)   Carry out a **TTESt**. Can you reject H_0 at the 5% significance level? At the 1% significance level?

(d)   Give a 90% confidence interval for the mean increase in listening score due to attending the summer institute.

(e)   Use the **STESt** command to assess whether the summer institute improves Spanish listening skills. Are your conclusions different from part (c)?

7.33   The data below are the survival times of 72 guinea pigs after they were injected with tubercle bacilli in a medical experiment. The distribution was found in Exercise 1.120 to be strongly skewed to the right. (Data from T. Bjerkedal, "Acquisition of resistance in guinea pigs infected with different doses of virulent tubercle bacilli," *American Journal of Hygiene*, 72 (1960), pp. 130–148.)

43	45	53	56	56	57	58	66	67	73
74	79	80	80	81	81	81	82	83	83
84	88	89	91	91	92	92	97	99	99
100	100	101	102	102	102	103	104	107	108
109	113	114	118	121	123	126	128	137	138
139	144	145	147	156	162	174	178	179	184
191	198	211	214	243	249	329	380	403	511
522	598								

(a)   Give a 95% confidence interval for the mean survival time by applying the **TINTerval** command to these data.

(b)   Use the **LET** command to transform the data by taking the logarithm of each value. Display the transformed data by a **HISTtogram** and a normal quantile plot. The distribution of the logarithms remains somewhat right-skewed, but is much closer to symmetry than the original distribution. Probability values from the *t* distribution will be more accurate for the transformed data.

(c)   Give a 95% confidence interval for the mean of the log survival time by applying the **TTESt** command to the transformed data.

7.44   A selective private college gives the Survey of Study Habits and Attitudes (SSHA) to an SRS of both male and female freshmen. The data for both men and women are given in SSHA.MTW. The data for the women are as follows:

154	109	137	115	152	140	154	178	101
103	126	126	137	165	165	129	200	148

Here are the scores of the men:

108	140	114	91	180	115	126	92	169	146
109	132	75	88	113	151	70	115	187	104

(a) Examine each sample graphically, with special attention to outliers and skewness. Is use of a t procedure acceptable for these data?

(b) Most studies have found that the mean SSHA score for men is lower than the mean score in a comparable group of women. Use the TWOSample t command to test this supposition here. Obtain a P-value, and give your conclusions.

(c) Give a 90% confidence interval for the mean difference between the SSHA scores of male and female freshmen at this college. This can also be done with the TWOSample t command by specifying a 90% level.

7.45 Plant scientists have developed varieties of corn that have increased amounts of the essential amino acid lysine. In a test of the protein quality of this corn, an experimental group of 20 one-day-old male chicks was fed a ration containing the new corn. A control group of another 20 chicks received a ration that was identical except that it contained normal corn. Below and in CORN.MTW are the weight gains (in grams) after 21 days. (Based on G. L. Cromwell et al., "A comparison of the nutritive value of *opaque-2, floury-2* and normal corn for the chick," *Poultry Science*, 47 (1968), pp. 840–847.)

Control				Experimental			
380	321	366	356	361	447	401	375
283	349	402	462	434	403	393	426
356	410	329	399	406	318	467	407
350	384	316	272	427	420	477	392
345	455	360	431	430	339	410	326

(a) Present the data graphically. Are there outliers or strong skewness that might prevent the use of t procedures?

(b) State the hypotheses for a statistical test of the claim that chicks fed high-lysine corn gain weight faster. Carry out the test using the TWOSample t command. Is the result significant at the 10% level? At the 5% level? At the 1% level?

(c) Give a 95% confidence interval for the mean extra weight gain in chicks fed high-lysine corn.

7.46 The table below and SYSTOLIC.MTW give data on the blood pressure before and after treatment for two groups of black males. One group took a calcium supplement, and the other group received a placebo.

Calcium group		Placebo group	
Begin	End	Begin	End
107	100	123	124
110	114	109	97
123	105	112	113
129	112	102	105
112	115	98	95
111	116	114	119
107	106	119	114
112	102	112	114
136	125	110	121
102	104	117	118
		130	133

(a)   Use the **LET** command to make two new columns for the blood pressure reductions for each subject in the two groups. Name the columns 'calcium' and 'placebo'. Perform a significance test using a **TWOSample t** test with the **POOLed** subcommand. This test requires equal population standard deviations.

(b)   Repeat the **TWOSample t** test without the **POOLed** subcommand. Compare your *P*-value with the result from (a).

(c)   Give a 90% confidence interval for the difference in means, again with and without the **POOLed** subcommand. How do the widths of your intervals compare?

7.47   CALORIES.MTW gives data on the calories in a sample of brands of each of three kinds of hot dogs.

(a)   Give a 95% confidence interval for the difference in mean calorie content between beef and poultry hot dogs. Can the hypothesis that the population means are equal be rejected at the 5% significance level?

(b)   What assumptions does your statistical procedure in (a) require? Which of these assumptions are justified or not important in this case? Are any of the assumptions doubtful in this case?

7.65   A selective private college gives the Survey of Study Habits and Attitudes (SSHA) to an SRS of both male and female freshmen. SSHA scores are generally less variable among women than among men. We want to know whether this is true for this college. The data are given in Exercise 7.44 and SSHA.MTW.

(a)   Verify that the SSHA distributions are close to normally distributed using the **NSCores** and **PLOT** commands.

(b)   Use the **LET** command to compute the test statistic for an *F* test. (The numerator s^2 belongs to the group that H_a claims to have the larger σ.)

(c)   Use the **CDF** command (no doubling of *p*) to obtain the *P*-value. Be sure the degrees of freedom are in the proper order. What do you conclude about the variation in SSHA scores?

7.79 A pharmaceutical manufacturer checks the potency of products during manufacture by chemical analysis. The standard release potency for cephalothin crystals is set at 910. An assay of the previous 16 lots gives the following potency data. The data are also stored in POTENCY.MTW.

| 897 | 914 | 913 | 906 | 916 | 918 | 905 | 921 |
| 918 | 906 | 895 | 893 | 908 | 906 | 907 | 901 |

(a) Check the data for outliers or strong skewness that might threaten the validity of the *t* procedures.

(b) Use the **TTESt** command to determine whether there is significant evidence at the 5% level that the mean potency is not equal to the standard release potency.

(c) Give a 95% confidence interval for the mean potency.

7.82 POLLUTION.MTW gives data on the concentration of airborne particulate matter in a rural area upwind from a small city and in the center of the city. We want to compare the mean level of particulates in the city and in the rural area. We suspect that pollution is higher in the city and hope to find evidence for this suspicion.

(a) State H_0 and H_a.

(b) Which type of *t* procedure is appropriate: one-sample, matched pairs, or two-sample?

(c) Make a graph to check for outliers or strong skewness that might prevent the use of *t* procedures. Your graph should reflect the type of procedure that you will use.

(d) Carry out the appropriate *t* test. Give the *P*-value and report your conclusion.

(e) Give a 90% confidence interval for the mean amount by which the city particulate level exceeds the rural level.

(f) The sign test allows us to assess whether city particulate levels are higher than nearby rural levels on the same day without the use of normal distributions. Carry out a sign test for the data in this exercise. State H_0 and H_a and give the *P*-value and your conclusion.

7.85 EARTH.MTW gives measurements of the density of the earth, made in 1798 by Henry Cavendish. Display the data graphically to check for skewness and outliers. Then give an estimate for the density of the earth from Cavendish's data and a margin of error for your estimate.

7.87 EXHAUST.MTW gives the levels of three pollutants in the exhaust of 46 randomly selected vehicles of the same type. You will investigate emissions of nitrogen oxides (NOX).

(a) Make a **STEM-and-leaf** diagram and a normal quantile plot of the NOX levels. Do the plots suggest that the distribution of NOX emissions is approximately normal? Can you safely employ *t* procedures to analyze these data?

(b)   Your supervisor would like the average NOX level to be less than 1 gram per mile. You will have to tell him that it's not so. Carry out a **TTESt** to assess the strength of the evidence that the mean NOX level is greater than 1, then write a short report to your supervisor based on your work. (Your supervisor never heard of *P*-values, so you must use plain language.)

(c)   Give a 99% confidence interval for the mean NOX level in the vehicles.

7.88   Is there a difference between the average SAT scores of males and females? The CSDATA.MTW data set gives the math (SATM) and verbal (SATV) scores for a group of 224 computer science majors. The data set is described in the data appendix (page 792) of *I.P.S.*

(a)   Perform the **TWOSample t** test to compare the average SATM scores of males and females. Is it appropriate to use the **POOLed** subcommand for this comparison? Summarize your results giving both versions of the *t* test and the *F* test for equality of standard deviations. Draw a conclusion and present your results graphically. Give a 99% confidence interval for the difference in the means.

(b)   Answer part (a) for the SAT verbal score.

(c)   The students in the CSDATA data set were all computer science majors entering as freshmen during a particular year. To what extent do you think that your results would generalize (i) to computer science students entering in different years; (ii) to computer science majors at other colleges and universities; (iii) to college students in general?

7.89   The WOOD.MTW data set described in the data appendix of I.P.S. (page 792) gives first (T1) and second (T2) measurements of the modulus of elasticity for 50 strips of wood. We would like to see if the process of taking the first measurement changes the strips in such a way that the second measurement will tend to be higher or lower than the first.

(a)   Use the **LET** command to compute the differences D = T1 - T2, and describe the distribution of D using graphical and numerical summaries.

(b)   Perform the **TTESt** of the null hypothesis that the mean of D is zero. Summarize your results and draw a conclusion.

(c)   Give a 95% confidence interval for the mean of D.

7.90   The READING.MTW data set is described in the data appendix (page 794) of *I.P.S.* The response variable POST3 is to be compared for three methods of teaching reading. The basal method is the standard or control method and the two new methods are DRTA and strategies. We can use the methods of this chapter to compare Basal with DRTA and Basal with Strat. Note that to make comparisons among three treatments it is more appropriate to use the procedures that we will learn in Chapter 10.

(a)   Is the mean reading score with the DRTA method higher than that for the basal method? Perform an analysis to answer this question and summarize your results.

(b)   Answer part (a) for Strat in place of DRTA.

Chapter 8
Inference for Count Data

Commands to be covered in this chapter:

STORe [in 'filename']

EXECute commands [in 'filename']

ECHO the commands that follow

NOECho the commands that follow

NOTE any commands may be put here

CHISquare analysis on frequency table in C,...,C

TABLe the data classified by C,...,C

Inference for Proportions

Minitab is designed to deal primarily with quantitative variables rather than the categorical variables considered in this chapter. There are no Minitab commands specifically designed to compute confidence intervals or significance tests for proportions.[*] However, we can do a simple modification of the one-sample procedures based on the z statistic that are described in Chapter 6. This can be done provided that n is large enough so that $\hat{p}$ has approximately a normal distribution.

If we enter a categorical variable so that a "success" (such as a "yes" answer to a question) is a 1 and a failure is a 0, then $\hat{p}$ can be computed as the mean of the data. For example, below we enter the data from Example 8.4 of *I.P.S.* The French naturalist Buffon tossed a coin 4040 times and obtained 2048 heads. The sample proportion is

$$\hat{p} = \frac{2048}{4040} = .5069$$

The same result is obtained using the **MEAN** command below. We will enter the data into C1 using repeat factors. These were previously introduced in Chapter 3. 2048(1) is equivalent to 2048 repetitions of 1.

---

[*] If you are using *The Student Edition of Minitab* (Version 8.0 or higher) from Addison-Wesley, the macro **PTEST** is available for performing significance tests and computing confidence intervals for single proportions.

```
MTB > set c1
DATA> 2048(1) 1992(0)
DATA> end
MTB > info

COLUMN      NAME        COUNT
C1                      4040

CONSTANTS USED: NONE

MTB > mean c1 k1
    MEAN    =     0.50693
```

Since we can think of a proportion as being the mean of a variable that takes only the values 0 and 1, we can use the **ZINTerval** and **ZTESt** commands to calculate confidence intervals and perform significance tests. Both of these Minitab commands require that a value of σ be specified. If a confidence interval is to be computed, then the appropriate value of the standard deviation is

$$\sigma = \sqrt{\hat{p}(1-\hat{p})}$$

Since $\hat{p}$ was stored in K1 above, we can easily compute the correct value of σ using the **LET** command as shown below.

```
MTB > let k2=sqrt(k1*(1-k1))
MTB > print k2
K2        0.499952
```

Now the **ZINTerval** command can be used to compute a 99% confidence interval for the population proportion.

```
MTB > zint 99 k2 c1

THE ASSUMED SIGMA =0.500

                N      MEAN    STDEV   SE MEAN    99.0 PERCENT C.I.
    C1        4040   0.50693  0.50001  0.00787  ( 0.48663, 0.52723)
```

If Buffon used a fair coin, then the proportion of heads would be 0.5. To assess whether the data provide evidence that the coin was not fair, we test

$$H_0: p = .5$$
$$H_a: p \neq .5$$

Significance tests for a population proportion can be performed using the **ZTESt** command. If we are testing the hypothesis $H_0: p = p_0$, then the appropriate value for the standard deviation is

$$\sigma = \sqrt{p_0(1-p_0)}$$

Below, we calculate the appropriate value of σ and then use it in the **ZTESt** command.

```
MTB > let k3 = sqrt(.5*(1-.5))
MTB > print k3
K3        0.5000
```

```
MTB > ztest .5 k3 c1

TEST OF MU = 0.50000 VS MU N.E. 0.50000
THE ASSUMED SIGMA = 0.500

                 N      MEAN    STDEV   SE MEAN        Z   P VALUE
C1            4040   0.50693  0.50001   0.00787     0.88      0.38
```

The STORe Command*

The **STORe** command stores Minitab commands into a macro file for later execution. The command format is

```
STORe [in 'filename']
```

Commands are entered at the STOR> prompt and the command **END** is used to stop storing commands. Macro files are useful for repeating a sequence of commands. If a filename is given, then commands are stored in the specified file with an .MTB extension. If no filename is given, then commands are stored in MINITAB.MTB. If you enter the commands **READ**, **SET**, or **INSErt**, you must not use **END** at the end of the data. If you do, Minitab will take this **END** of data as the end of the stored instructions.

The EXECute Command

The **EXECute** command executes commands stored in the specified macro file and has the following format.

```
EXECute commands [in 'filename']
```

If a filename is given, then commands are executed from the specified file with the MTB finename extension. If no filename is given, then commands are executed from MINITAB.MTB.

Below is a simple example. Each month a researcher collects data from 20 plants. The ten variables of interest are entered into Minitab columns 1 through 10. The statistical analysis is rather long, so she would like to write the commands just once, store them in a file, and **EXECute** the file each time she has new data. She would use

```
MTB > STORE 'PLANTS'
STOR> HISTOGRAM C1-C10
STOR> DESCRIBE C1-C10
STOR>    (other commands, ...)
MTB > END
```

---

* The following sections describing the **STORe**, **EXECute**, **ECHO**, **NOECho**, and **NOTE** commands contain advanced material and may be skipped.

Now suppose next month she gets some new data. She would use

```
MTB > READ C1-C10
DATA>   (data)
DATA> END
MTB > EXECUTE 'PLANTS'
```

Once you have created a command file, you can execute it in the current Minitab session or in a later session. A special feature, called the CK capability, makes macros very flexible. The integer part of a column number may be replaced by a stored constant. This is illustrated in the following example.

```
MTB > LET K1 = 5
MTB > PRINT C1-CK1
```

Since K1 = 5, this prints C1 through C5.

The ECHO, NOECho, and NOTE Commands

The commands **ECHO** and **NOECho** control the echo printing of Minitab commands in the output. When you execute a macro file, the commands are normally displayed or echoed. If you do not want them displayed, use the **NOECho** command. Then only output and **NOTE** lines will be displayed. Use the command **ECHO** to restore display of commands.

The **NOTE** command provides a way to put notes on the output during the execution of a command file (macro). Unlike other commands, the **NOTE** command is echoed (in a special way) when the **NOECho** command is in effect. In **NOECho** mode, the command prompt (the "MTB >") and the first five characters of the **NOTE** command line (normally "NOTE ") are not echoed. The following example illustrates the **NOTE**, **NOECho**, and **ECHO** commands.

```
STOR> NOECHO
STOR> NOTE Enter the desired mean:
STOR> READ 'TERMINAL' C10;
STOR> NOBS = 1.
STOR> LET  K1 = C10(1)
STOR> RANDOM 100 C1;
STOR> NORMAL K1 1.
STOR> END
```

The output will contain

```
Enter the desired mean:
DATA>
```

The terminal then waits for you to respond. TERMINAL is a special filename that allows the data to be entered interactively. A semicolon (;) is used at the end of the command to indicate that a subcommand will follow. The subcommand **NOBS** tells **READ** how many numbers to expect. This means the user of the macro does not have to type the command **END** to signal the end of typing data. The period (.) indicates that the subcommands have been completed. C1 will then contain 100 random normal observations with the mean specified by the user.

The macro capability is used below for comparing two population proportions. The following example creates a command file called TWOP.MTB to test $H_0: p_1 = p_2$. We compute the z statistic

$$z = \frac{\hat{p}_1 - \hat{p}_2}{s_p(D)}$$

where

$$s_p(D) = \sqrt{\hat{p}(1 - \hat{p})\left(\frac{1}{n_1} + \frac{1}{n_2}\right)} \quad \text{and} \quad \hat{p} = \frac{X_1 + X_2}{n_1 + n_2}$$

Once the z statistic is computed, the P-value is computed using the **CDF** command.

```
MTB > store 'TWOP'
STOR> noecho
STOR> note   This macro calculates the test statistic and p-value for
STOR> note   comparing two population proportions.  The data are stored
STOR> note   in two columns with 1 indicating "success"
STOR> note   and 0 indicating "failure".
STOR> note
STOR> note   At the "DATA" prompt below, enter the column numbers to be
STOR> note   compared.  If the data are in C1 and C2, enter 1 and 2.
STOR> set 'terminal' c10;
STOR> nobs = 2.
STOR> copy c10 k11 k12
STOR> note Data from first column:
STOR> mean ck11 k13
STOR> n ck11 k14
STOR> note Data from second column:
STOR> mean ck12 k15
STOR> n ck12 k16
STOR> let k17 = (k13*k14+k15*k16)/(k14+k16)
STOR> let k18 = sqrt(k17*(1-k17)*(1/k14+1/k16))
STOR> let k19 = (k13-k15)/k18
STOR> cdf k19   k20
STOR> let c10(1) = k20
STOR> let c10(2) = 1- c10(1)
STOR> let k12 = min(c10)
STOR> let k13=k12*2
STOR> note   The z-statistic value is
STOR> print k19
STOR> note   The p-value for a one-tailed test is
STOR> print k12
STOR> note The p-value for a two-tailed test is
STOR> print k13
STOR> end
```

You can also create or edit macro files with an editor. Be sure to save it in standard (ASCII) format, and name it with the three-letter filename extension MTB.

Example 8.9 of *I.P.S.* considers a one-sided test to examine whether rural households that display Christmas trees are more likely than urban households to choose natural Christmas trees. The survey responses show that 89 of 261 urban households and 64 of 160 rural households chose a natural tree. The data have been stored in TREES.MTW so that "1" indicates a natural tree and "0" an artificial tree.

```
MTB > info

COLUMN      NAME       COUNT
C1          Urban      261
C2          Rural      160

CONSTANTS USED: NONE
```

The macro **TWOP** can be executed as illustrated below.

```
MTB > execute 'twop'
This macro calculates the test statistic and p-value for
comparing two population proportions.  The data are stored
in two columns with 1 indicating "success"
and 0 indicating "failure".

At the "DATA" prompt below, enter the column numbers to be
compared.  If the data are in C1 and C2, enter 1 and 2.
DATA> 1 2
Data from first column:
   MEAN     =       0.34100
   N        =       261
Data from second column:
   MEAN     =       0.40000
   N        =       160
 The z-statistic value is
K19      -1.22177
 The p-value for a one-tailed test is
K12       0.110898
The p-value for a two-tailed test is
K13       0.221796
```

The CHISquare Command

The **CHISquare** command does a χ^2 test of the null hypothesis that there is "no relationship" between the column variable and the row variable in a two-way table. The command format is

```
CHISquare analysis on frequency table in C,...,C
```

The command performs a χ^2 test for independence or association on a frequency table which has already been formed and stored in the worksheet. You may specify up to seven columns. The columns must contain integer values. Below, we will illustrate the **CHISquare** command on the data from Example 8.14 in *I.P.S.* The 356 subjects are classified according to their socioeconomic status (high, middle, and low) and their smoking habits (current smokers, former smokers, or those who had never smoked). The data table is shown below.

Smoking	Socioeconomic Status			Total
	High	Middle	Low	
Current	51	22	43	116
Former	92	21	28	141
Never	68	9	22	99
Total	211	52	93	356

The data from this table are entered below and then the **CHISquare** command is illustrated.

```
MTB > set c1
DATA> 51 92 68
DATA> set c2
DATA> 22 21 9
DATA> set c3
DATA> 43 28 22
DATA> end
MTB > name c1 'high' c2 'middle' c3 'low'
MTB > chis c1 c2 c3

Expected counts are printed below observed counts

          high    middle      low     Total
    1       51        22       43       116
          68.75     16.94    30.30

    2       92        21       28       141
          83.57     20.60    36.83

    3       68         9       22        99
          58.68     14.46    25.86

Total      211        52       93       356

ChiSq =   4.584 +   1.509 +   5.320 +
          0.850 +   0.008 +   2.119 +
          1.481 +   2.062 +   0.577 = 18.510
df = 4
```

The **CHISquare** command provides the χ^2 statistic and the number of degrees of freedom. The *P*-value can be obtained using the **CDF** (cumulative distribution function) command with the **CHISquare** subcommand. The subcommand format is

```
CHISquare with df = K
```

The number of degrees of freedom for the χ^2 statistic is equal to

$$(\text{number of rows} - 1) \times (\text{number of columns} - 1)$$

The **CDF** command calculates the probability that an observation is less than or equal to a specified value. Therefore, the *P*-value is equal to 1 minus the probability value that is printed. Below, we calculate the probability that a χ^2 with 4 degrees of freedom is less than 18.510.

```
MTB > cdf 18.510;
SUBC> chis 4.
    18.5100    0.9990
```

The value obtained is 0.9990, so the *P*-value for the above test of independence is 0.001. There is strong evidence of an association between smoking and SES.

The **TABLe** Command

In the previous section the two-way table was already prepared; all we had to do was compute the value of χ^2 and the *P*-value. Minitab can also be used to make the table and then do the chi-square test all in one operation. The procedure is a simple extension of the one discussed in Chapter 2 for making tables.

Consider again the job offer data for the 120 applicants considered in Chapter 2 and found in JOBS.MTW. We used the command **TABLe** to make a table that classified applicants by sex and decision. The same command will do a chi-square analysis, if we add the **CHISquare** subcommand

```
CHISquare test [output code = K]
```

Notice that the subcommand format is different from the one used above with the **CDF** command. Here, it is not necessary to specify the number of degrees of freedom. The output code, K, on the **CHISquare** subcommand puts additional statistics in each cell. If K=1 (the default), just the count is put in each cell. If K=2, the count and expected count are given (as with the **CHISquare** command). When the **TABLe** command with the **CHISquare** subcommand is used, the *P*-value is not provided. The **CDF** command is used below to compute the *P*-value for this example.

```
MTB > table 'sex' by 'offer';
SUBC> chisquare 2.


   ROWS: sex      COLUMNS: offer

              · 0       1      ALL

     0        40       25       65
            37.92    27.08    65.00

     1        30       25       55
            32.08    22.92    55.00

   ALL       70       50      120
            70.00    50.00   120.00

CHI-SQUARE =       0.599   WITH D.F. =     1

   CELL CONTENTS --
                    COUNT
                    EXP FREQ

MTB > cdf .599;
SUBC> chis 1.
    0.5990     0.5610
```

In the above example, the number of degrees of freedom is equal to 1 and the *P*-value is 0.4390, computed from $1 - P(\chi^2 < 0.5990) = 1 - 0.5610$.

EXERCISES

8.4   Large trees growing near power lines can cause power failures during storms when their branches fall on the lines. Power companies spend a great deal of time and money trimming and removing trees to prevent this problem. Researchers are developing hormone and chemical treatments that will stunt or slow tree growth. If the treatment is too severe, however, the tree will die. In one series of laboratory experiments on 216 sycamore trees, 41 trees died. These data are stored in SYCAMORE.MTW.

(a)   Use the **MEAN** command to calculate the sample proportion, $\hat{p}$.

(b)   The **ZINTerval** command can be used to calculate confidence intervals if the appropriate value of σ is used. Use the **LET** command to calculate this value of σ.

(c)   Use the **ZINTerval** command to calculate a 99% confidence interval for the proportion of trees that would be expected to die from this particular treatment.

(d)   Develop a macro to calculate confidence intervals for a single proportion. Check that your macro gives results that are consistent with (c).

8.14 LeRoy, a starting player for a major college basketball team, made only 40% of his free throws last season. During the summer he worked on developing a softer shot in the hope of improving his free-throw accuracy. In the first eight games of this season LeRoy made 25 free throws in 40 attempts. Let p be his probability of making each free throw he shoots this season.

(a)   State the null hypothesis H_0 that LeRoy's free-throw probability has remained the same as last year and the alternative H_a that his work in the summer resulted in a higher probability of success.

(b)   If you are using *The Student Edition of MINITAB*, used the `PTEST` macro to test H_0 versus H_a. If you are using another version of Minitab, test the hypothesis using the `ZTESt` command. Do you accept or reject H_0 for $\alpha = 0.05$? Find the *P*-value.

(c)   Give a 90% confidence interval for LeRoy's free-throw success probability for the new season. (This can be done using either the `PTEST` macro if you are using *The Student Edition of MINITAB* or the `ZINTerval` command.) Are you convinced that he is now a better free-throw shooter than last season?

8.21   In the 1991 regular baseball season, the World Series Champion Minnesota Twins played 81 games at home and 81 games away. They won 51 of their home games and 44 of the games played away. These data are stored in TWINS.MTW. We can consider these games as samples from potentially large populations of games played at home and away. Do these samples provide strong evidence in favor of a home-field advantage?

(a)   Use the `TWOP` macro to test H_0 (that the Twins are equally likely to win at home or away) versus H_a (that the Twins are more likely to win at home). Give the appropriate *P*-value and state your conclusion.

(b)   Write a macro that can be used to compute a confidence interval for the difference between the probability that the Twins win at home and the probability that they win when on the road. Use the macro to compute a 90% confidence interval.

8.36   Investors use many "indicators" in their attempts to predict the behavior of the stock market. One of these is the "January indicator." Some investors believe that if the market is up in January, then it will be up for the rest of the year. On the other hand, if it is down in January, then it will be down for the rest of the year. The following table and STOCK.MTW give the data for the Standard and Poor's 500 stock index during the 75 years from 1916 to 1990:

Rest of	January	
the year	Up	Down
Up	35	13
Down	13	14

These data do not strictly conform to either of the sampling models described in this section. However, the chi-square analysis is valid for this problem if we assume that the yearly data are independent observations on a process that generates either an "up" or a "down" both in January and for the rest of the year.

(a) Use the **TABLe** command with the **COLPercents** subcommand. Explain briefly what the column percents for this table express.

(b) Repeat (a) with the **ROWPercents** subcommand.

(c) State appropriate null and alternative hypotheses for this problem. Use words rather than symbols.

(d) Use the **TABLe** command with the **CHISquare** subcommand to find the chi-square statistic and its degrees of freedom.

(e) Use the **CDF** command to calculate the *P*-value. What do you conclude?

(f) Write a short discussion of the evidence for the January indicator, referring to your analysis for substantiation.

8.38 A survey on the severity of rodent problems in commercial poultry houses studied a random sample of poultry operations. Each operation were classified by type (egg or turkey production) and by the extent of the rodent problems. Below and in POULTRY.MTW are the results of the classification.

Type	Mild	Moderate	Severe
Egg	34	33	7
Turkey	22	22	4

(a) The type of poultry operation is a natural explanatory variable. Calculate a **TABLe** of percents that describes how rodent problems vary with the type of operation. Summarize the results in words.

(b) State H_0 and H_a for this problem.

(c) Conduct a significance test for your hypotheses and give the results. What do you conclude?

8.39 Do businesses of different sizes respond more or less readily to questionnaires sent out by business schools? A study sent questionnaires to 200 randomly selected businesses of each of three sizes. Here are data on the responses. These data are also stored in BUSINESS.MTW. Note that the column sums are fixed by the design of the survey.

	Size		
	Small	Medium	Large
Response	125	81	40
No response	75	119	160
Total	200	200	200

(a) Use the **TABLe** command and the **COLPercent** subcommand to find the percent that responded and the percent that did not respond for each size of business. In what way do the response rates appear to vary with the size of the business?

(b) State in words an appropriate H_0 for this problem. What is H_a?

(c) Test your hypothesis using the **TABLe** command and the **CHISquare** subcommand. Give a full report of your conclusions.

8.42   Alcohol and nicotine consumption during pregnancy may harm children. Because drinking and smoking behaviors may be related, it is important to understand the nature of this relationship when assessing the possible effects on children. One study classified 452 mothers according to their alcohol intake prior to pregnancy recognition and their nicotine intake during pregnancy. The data are summarized in the following table. (Data from Ann P. Streissguth et al., "Intrauterine alcohol and nicotine exposure: attention and reaction time in 4-year-old children," *Developmental Psychology*, 20 (1984), pp. 533-541.)

| | Nicotine (mg/day) | | |
Alcohol (ounces/day)	None	1-15	16 or more
None	105	7	11
.01-.10	58	5	13
.11-.99	84	37	42
1.00 or more	57	16	17

(a)   Enter the data into three columns of a Minitab worksheet.
(b)   State in words an appropriate H_0 for this problem. What is H_a?
(c)   Test your hypothesis using the **CHISquare** and **CDF** commands.

8.50   In a study on blood pressure and diet, a random sample of Seventh Day Adventists were interviewed at a national meeting. Because many people who belong to this denomination are vegetarians, they are a very useful group for studying the effects of a meatless diet. Blacks in the population as a whole have a higher average blood pressure than whites. A study of this type should therefore take race into account in the analysis. The 312 people in the sample were categorized by race and whether or not they were vegetarians. The data are given in the following table and in SEVENTH.MTW. (Data provided by Chris Melby and David Goldflies, Department of Physical Education, Health, and Recreation Studies, Purdue University.)

Diet	Black	White
Vegetarian	42	135
Not vegetarian	47	88

Are the proportions of vegetarians the same among all black and white Seventh Day Adventists who attended this meeting?
(a)   Use the **TABLe** command to analyze the data, paying particular attention to this question. Include a **CHISquare** test in your analysis. Summarize your analysis and conclusions. What can you infer about the proportions of vegetarians among black and white Seventh Day Adventists in general?
(b)   **UNSTack** the data using the subscripts in the column labled 'Race'. Use the **TWOP** macro to test whether the proportions of vegetarians among

black and white Seventh Day Adventists are the same or different. Compare the results (especially the *P*-value) with those obtained in part (a).

8.54 Are there sex differences in the progress of students in doctoral programs? A major university classified all students entering Ph.D. programs in a given year by their status 6 years later. The categories were completed the degree, still enrolled, and dropped out. Here are the data.

Status	Men	Women
Completed	423	98
Still enrolled	134	33
Dropped out	238	98

Assume that these data can be viewed as a random sample giving us information on the process that students encounter when working toward a doctorate.
(a) Enter the data into two columns of a Minitab worksheet.
(b) State in words a null hypothesis and alternative that address the question of sex differences.
(c) Test your hypothesis using the CHISquare and CDF commands. Summarize your conclusions. What other factors not given might be relevant to this study?

8.59 Upper Wabash Tech has two professional schools, business and law. The data given below and in WABASH.MTW concern Upper Wabash Tech's two professional schools, business and law, and admission rates for male and female applicants.

	Business				Law	
	Admit	Deny			Admit	Deny
Male	480	120	Male		10	90
Female	180	20	Female		100	200

(a) Apply the chi-square test to the data for all applicants combined and summarize the results. This can be done with the TABLe command using data in columns 'sex' and 'admit'.
(b) The TABLe command can also be used (with 3 columns specified) to run separate chi-square analyses for business and law students. Summarize these results.
(c) Use the CDF command to determine whether the effects that illustrate Simpson's paradox in this example are statistically significant.

8.69 A recent study of 865 college students found that 42.5% had student loans. The students were randomly selected from the approximately 30,000 undergraduates enrolled in a large public university. The overall purpose of the study was to examine the effects of student loan burdens on the choice of a career. A student with a large debt may be more likely to choose a field where starting salaries are high so that the loan can more easily be repaid. The following table classifies the students by field of study and whether or not they have a loan. The data are also stored in LOAN.MTW. (Data provided by Susan Prohofsky, from her Ph.D. dissertation, *Selection of undergraduate major: the influence of expected costs and expected benefits*, Purdue University, 1991.)

Field of Study	Student loan	
	Yes	No
Agriculture	32	35
Child Development and Family Studies	37	50
Engineering	98	137
Liberal Arts and Education	89	124
Management	24	51
Science	31	29
Technology	57	71

(a)   State in words an appropriate H_0 for this problem. What is H_a?

(b)   Test your hypothesis using the **CHISquare** and **CDF** commands.

8.70   In the study described in the previous exercise, students were asked to respond to some questions regarding their interests and attitudes. Some of these questions form a scale called PEOPLE that measures altruism or an interest in the welfare of others. Each students was classified as low, medium, or high on this scale. Is there an association between PEOPLE score and field of study? The data are given below and stored in PEOPLE.MTW.

Field of study	PEOPLE score		
	Low	Medium	High
Agriculture	5	27	35
Child Development and Family Studies	1	32	54
Engineering	12	129	94
Liberal Arts and Education	7	77	129
Management	3	44	28
Science	7	29	24
Technology	2	62	64

(a)   State in words an appropriate H_0 for this problem. What is H_a?

(b)   Test your hypothesis using the **CHISquare** and **CDF** commands.

8.73   The proportion of women entering many professions has undergone considerable change in recent years. A study of students enrolled in pharmacy programs describes the changes in this field. A random sample of 700 students in their third or higher year of study at colleges of pharmacy was taken in each of several years. WOMEN.MTW and the following table give the numbers of women in each of these samples. (Data are based on *Seventh Report to the President and Congress on the Status of Health Personnel in the United States*, Public Health Service, 1990.)

Year	Number of women
1970	164
1972	195
1974	226
1976	283
1978	302
1980	343
1982	369
1984	384
1986	412

(a)   Use the **CHISquare** test to assess the change in the percentage of women pharmacy students over time and summarize your results. (You will need to use the **LET** command to calculate the number of male students for each year using the fact that the sample size each year is 700.)

(b)   **PLOT** the percentage of women versus year. Describe the plot. Is it roughly linear? Find the least-squares **REGRession** line that summarizes the relation between time and the percentage of women pharmacy students. Would you be willing to use this line to predict the percentage of women pharmacy students in the year 2000? Explain why or why not.

Chapter 9
Inference for Regression

Commands to be covered in this chapter:

REGRess C on K predictors C,...,C
BRIEf [with output code = K] for commands that follow
CORRelate the data in C,...,C

The REGRess Command

To begin with in this chapter we will consider simple linear regression. In Chapter 2, the command format for the **REGRess** command was given as

REGRess C on 1 predictor C

This command format is appropriate only for simple linear regression. If multiple regression is required, as in the later part of the chapter, the number of predictor variables is specified (instead of 1) followed by columns containing the predictors. This will be described later in the chapter. In Example 9.1 of *I.P.S.* the relationship between body density (y) and the logarithm of skinfold thickness (x) is examined. The data are stored in DENSITY.MTW in columns named DEN and LSKIN. A model of the form

$$y_i = \beta_0 + \beta_1 x_i + \varepsilon_i \qquad i = 1,2,\ldots,n$$

is developed, where ε_i is assumed to be independent and normally distributed with mean 0 and standard deviation σ. This is the same as the least-squares line $\hat{y} = a + bx$, introduced in Chapter 2, except that we now use Greek letters to indicate that the slope and intercept are population parameters. The estimates for β_0, β_1, and σ (b_0, b_1, and s) can be found using the **REGRess** command. First we examine the variables and their relationship. The **DESCribe** command should be used to determine the mean and standard deviation of the variables and the **PLOT** command should be used to produce a scatterplot of the data. Since the relationship appears to be linear (Figure 9.4 of *I.P.S.*), we proceed with the **REGRESS** command as shown below.

```
MTB > regr c2 1 c1

The regression equation is
DEN = 1.16 - 0.0632 LSKIN

Predictor        Coef       Stdev     t-ratio        p
Constant      1.16310     0.00649      179.20    0.000
LSKIN        -0.063202    0.004101     -15.41    0.000

s = 0.008446    R-sq = 72.5%    R-sq(adj) = 72.2%

Analysis of Variance

SOURCE        DF          SS          MS         F         p
Regression     1      0.016944    0.016944    237.51    0.000
Error         90      0.006420    0.000071
Total         91      0.023364

Unusual Observations
Obs.    LSKIN        DEN       Fit  Stdev.Fit   Residual    St.Resid
   9     1.50    1.08855   1.06810    0.00092    0.02045       2.44R
  23     1.87    1.02648   1.04466    0.00153   -0.01818      -2.19R
  42     1.38    1.09563   1.07572    0.00116    0.01991       2.38R
  51     2.08    1.03853   1.03163    0.00228    0.00690       0.85 X
  61     1.50    1.09190   1.06839    0.00093    0.02351       2.80R
  70     1.79    1.07222   1.05021    0.00126    0.02201       2.63R
  76     1.00    1.09634   1.09982    0.00249   -0.00348      -0.43 X

R denotes an obs. with a large st. resid.
X denotes an obs. whose X value gives it large influence.
```

The values of b_1 and b_0 are given in the column labeled Coef. The column labeled Predictor tells us that the first entry, Constant, is b_0 and the second, LSKIN, is b_1. We see that $b_0 = 1.16310$ and $b_1 = -0.063202$. These are the estimates of β_0 and β_1. These values are rounded and appear in the regression equation.

```
DEN = 1.16 - 0.0632 LSKIN
```

The estimate of σ is given as $s = 0.008446$. The sum of squared residuals is found in the Analysis of Variance section in the column labeled SS and the row marked Error. The value is 0.00642. The degrees of freedom for this sum of squares are found in the same row in the column marked DF. Because $n = 92$, there are $n - 2 = 90$ degrees of freedom. The value of s^2 (0.000071) is found in the same row in the column labeled MS and is equal to 0.00642/90. The square root of this value is the estimated standard deviation, s, given above.

The BRIEf Command

The BRIEf command controls the amount of output printed from the REGRess command. The command has the following format.

```
BRIEf [with output code = K] for commands that follow
```

The larger the value of K, the more output. K = 0 turns off all screen output except for error messages. This is useful for executing macros where you don't want to see intermediate results. For K = 1, the regression equation, table of coefficients, *s*, R-squared, R-squared adjusted, and the first part of the analysis of variance table are displayed. For K = 2, in addition to the output from BRIEf 1, the second part of the analysis of variance table, the "unusual" observations in the table of fits and residuals are displayed. Brief 2 is the default output, that is, what you get if no **BRIEf** command has been given. If K = 3, in addition to the output from BRIEf 2, the full table of fits and residuals is displayed.

In the example above, we have fitted a line and we should now examine the residuals. Recall from Chapter 2 that the residuals can be obtained using the **RESIduals** subcommand with the following format.

```
RESIduals put into C
```

The **NSCOres** and **PLOT** commands are used below to produce a normal quantile plot of the residuals. In addition, the **BRIEf** command is illustrated with K = 1.

```
MTB > brief 1
MTB > regr c2 1 c1;
SUBC> resid c3.

The regression equation is
DEN = 1.16 - 0.0632 LSKIN

Predictor        Coef        Stdev      t-ratio          p
Constant      1.16310      0.00649       179.20      0.000
LSKIN        -0.063202     0.004101       -15.41      0.000

s = 0.008446     R-sq = 72.5%      R-sq(adj) = 72.2%

Analysis of Variance

SOURCE          DF          SS          MS          F          p
Regression       1      0.016944    0.016944     237.51      0.000
Error           90      0.006420    0.000071
Total           91      0.023364
```

```
MTB > name c3 'resid'
MTB > nscores c3 c4
MTB > name c4 'nscores'
MTB > plot c4 c3
```

```
  nscores -                                                           *
          -                                                         *
          -                                                      **
     1.6+                                          *  **
          -                                       *4
          -                                    4*  2
          -                                 *4*  4
          -                              *433
     0.0+                            *73*
          -                         *523
          -                    22*23
          -                 24*
          -              *3  *
    -1.6+          *2
          -          **
          -         *
          -     *
          ------+---------+---------+---------+---------+---------+resid
           -0.0160   -0.0080    0.0000    0.0080    0.0160    0.0240
```

Since the plot looks fairly straight, the assumption of normally distributed residuals appears to be reasonable. This is important for the inference that follows.

Confidence Intervals and Hypothesis Tests for β_0 and β_1

Confidence intervals and tests for the slope and intercept are based on the normal sampling distributions of the estimates b_1 and b_0. Since the standard deviations are not known, a t distribution is used. The value of s_{b_1} appears in the output from the **REGRess** command to the right of the estimated slope, $b_1 = -0.063202$; it is 0.004101. Similarly, the value of s_{b_0} appears to the right of the estimated constant, $b_0 = 1.16310$; it is 0.00649. Confidence intervals for b_0 and b_1 have the form

$$\text{estimate} \pm t^* s_{\text{estimate}}$$

That is, $\beta_1 = b_1 \pm t^* s_{b_1}$, where t^* is the upper $(1-C)/2$ critical value for the $t(n-2)$ distribution. The value of t^* can be calculated using the **INVCdf** command. For example, for a 95% confidence interval, $C = 0.95$.

```
MTB > invcdf .025;
SUBC> t 90.
    0.0250   -1.9867
```

Therefore, the value of t^* is 1.9867. The upper and lower bounds for the confidence interval can be calculated using the **LET** command as shown below.

```
MTB > let k1 = -.0632+1.9867*.0041
MTB > let k2 = -.0632-1.9867*.0041
MTB > print k1 k2
K1        -0.0550545
K2        -0.0713455
```

Therefore, a 95% confidence interval for β_1 is (−0.0714,−0.0551) as given in *I.P.S.* The t statistic and P-value for the test of

$$H_0 : \beta_1 = 0$$

$$H_a : \beta_1 \neq 0$$

appear in the columns labeled t-ratio and p. The *t* ratio can also be obtained from the formula

$$t = \frac{b_1}{s_{b_1}} = \frac{-.0632}{.0041} = -15.41$$

The *P*-value is listed as 0.000. This means that the *P*-value is less than 0.001. There is strong evidence against the null hypothesis. Confidence intervals and hypothesis tests for β_0 can be obtained similarly.

The PREDict Subcommand

The **PREDict** subcommand computes estimates of fitted *Y*'s for given values of the explanatory variables. It prints out a table that contains the fitted *Y* values, standard deviation of the fitted *Y*-values, a 95% confidence interval, and a 95% prediction interval. The subcommand format is given below.

```
PREDict for E,...,E
```

The explanatory variables may be specified as constants such as 68 or K3, or as columns containing a list of values. Up to 10 **PREDict** subcommands can be used with one **REGRess** command. For example:

```
MTB > regr c2 1 c1;
SUBC> pred 1.266.
```

(same regression output as above)

```
     Fit   Stdev.Fit        95% C.I.             95% P.I.
 1.08309     0.00152   (1.08007,1.08611)   (1.06604,1.10014)
```

The value given in the column labeled Fit is the value of DEN given by the equation DEN = 1.16 − 0.0632 LSKIN, when LSKIN = 1.266. The value given in the column labeled Stdev.Fit is $s_{y(x^*)}$. The output from the **REGRess** command also gives these values, but only for unusual observations.

The interval listed under the 95% C.I. column is the confidence interval for the mean response. It is computed as $\hat{\mu}_{y(x^*)} \pm t^* s_{y(x^*)}$, where $\hat{\mu}_{y(x^*)}$ is 1.08309 and t^* is the upper $(1-C)/2$ critical value for the $t(n-2)$ distribution with $C = 95$.

The interval listed under the 95% P.I. column is the prediction interval for a future observation. It is computed as $\hat{y} \pm t^* s_{\hat{y}}$, where $\hat{y}$ is 1.08309 and t^* is the upper $(1-C)/2$ critical value for the $t(n-2)$ distribution with $C = 95$. $s_{\hat{y}}$ is larger than $s_{y(x^*)}$ and is easily calculated from the following formula.

$$s_{\hat{y}}^2 = s^2 + s_{y(x^*)}^2$$

Analysis of Variance for Regression*

The analysis of variance table produced by the **REGRess** command gives the same calculations as the analysis of variance (ANOVA) table given in section 9.1 (page 658) of *I.P.S.* The format is slightly different and is illustrated below.

Analysis of Variance

SOURCE	DF	SS	MS	F	p
Regression	1	$\Sigma(\hat{y}_i - \bar{y})^2$	MSM=SSM/DFM	MSM/MSE	
Error	$n-2$	$\Sigma(y_i - \hat{y}_i)^2$	MSE=SSE/DFE		
Total	$n-1$	$\Sigma(y_i - \bar{y})^2$	MST=SST/DFT		

The value of the F statistic in the output given earlier is 237.51. This is the test statistic for

$$H_0: \beta_1 = 0$$
$$H_a: \beta_1 \neq 0$$

In the earlier output, the value given in the column marked p is 0.000. This means that the P-value, that is, the probability that a random variable having the $F(1, n-2)$ distribution is greater than or equal to 237.51, is less than 0.001. Therefore, there is strong evidence against the null hypothesis.

The CORRelate Command**

The **CORRelate** command calculates the correlation coefficient between each pair of variables. The command format is given below.

```
CORRelate the data in C,...,C
```

If more than two columns are specified, then the correlation is calculated between every pair of variables. The lower triangle of the resulting correlation matrix is displayed. If

---

* This optional material presents material that is needed for multiple regression.

** This material is optional and can be omitted without loss of continuity.

some data are missing, the correlations between each pair of columns are calculated using all rows that do not have either value missing. That is, the correlation matrix is calculated using "pairwise deletion" of missing values. The **CORRelate** command accepts up to 100 variables. Below we illustrate the command with the gas consumption data from Example 9.7 of *I.P.S.* The data are stored in CONSUME.MTW.

```
MTB > corr c1 c2

Correlation of x and y = 0.989
```

The **CORRelation** command does not perform the test

$$H_0: \rho = 0$$
$$H_a: \rho \neq 0$$

However, it is easy to use the **LET** command to compute the *t* statistic

$$t = \frac{r\sqrt{n-2}}{\sqrt{1-r^2}}$$

The **CDF** command can then be used to find the *P*-value. Below, we calculate the test statistic and use the **CDF** command.

```
MTB > let k1 = .989
MTB > let k2 = k1*sqrt(9-2)/sqrt(1-k1**2)
MTB > cdf k2;
SUBC> t 7.
   17.6902    1.0000
```

Since the **CDF** command calculates the probability that an observation is less than or equal to 17.69, the *P*-value is less than 0.0001. Thus, there is strong evidence against the null hypothesis.

Multiple Regression

As we mentioned at the beginning of this chapter, if multiple regression is required, the number of predictor variables must be specified in the **REGRess** command. In this case, the command format is

```
REGRess C on K predictors C,...,C
```

The command fits the regression equation

$$\mu_y = \beta_0 + \beta_1 X_1 + \beta_2 X_2 + \cdots + \beta_k X_k$$

to data in selected response and predictor variables. The response variable is specified first. The number of predictors is given next followed by columns containing the predictors. If the **PREDict** subcommand is used, you must specify one value for each predictor in the regression equation. To control the amount of printed output, use the command **BRIEf**.

We will illustrate the **REGRess** command with the data from Example 9.14 of *I.P.S.* The data concern 224 freshmen computer science majors and are stored in CSDATA.MTW and are described in the data appendix of *I.P.S.* The purpose of the study was to attempt to predict success in the early university years as measured by grade point average (GPA). We will consider three predictor variables ($p = 3$). The predictors are high school grades in mathematics (HSM), science (HSS), and English (HSE). The high school grades are coded on a scale from 1 to 10, with 10 corresponding to A, 9 to A−, 8 to B+, and so on.

The first step in the analysis is to examine each of the variables. Below, we use the **DESCribe** command on all four variables. The **HISTogram** and **STEM-and-leaf** commands can also be used to examine the shape of their distributions.

```
MTB > desc c1-c7

                N       MEAN     MEDIAN    TRMEAN      STDEV     SEMEAN
gpa           224     4.6352     4.7400    4.6738     0.7794     0.0521
hsm           224     8.321      9.000     8.455      1.639      0.109
hss           224     8.089      8.000     8.198      1.700      0.114
hse           224     8.094      8.000     8.183      1.508      0.101

                MIN       MAX        Q1        Q3
gpa          2.1200    6.0000    4.1625    5.2175
hsm          2.000    10.000     7.000    10.000
hss          3.000    10.000     7.000    10.000
hse          3.000    10.000     7.000     9.000
```

The second step in the analysis is to examine the relationships between all pairs of variables. Below, we use the **CORRelate** command to examine the relationships. Scatterplots can be produced using the **PLOT** command. (Plots are often more informative than the numerical summaries.)

```
MTB > corr c1-c6

             gpa       hsm       hss
hsm        0.436
hss        0.329     0.576
hse        0.289     0.447     0.579
```

To further explore the relationship between the explanatory variables and GPA, we can run the following multiple regression.

```
MTB > regr c1 3 c2-c4;
SUBC> resid c10.

The regression equation is
gpa = 2.59 + 0.169 hsm + 0.0343 hss + 0.0451 hse

Predictor        Coef       Stdev      t-ratio        p
Constant       2.5899      0.2942        8.80      0.000
hsm           0.16857     0.03549        4.75      0.000
hss           0.03432     0.03756        0.91      0.362
hse           0.04510     0.03870        1.17      0.245

s = 0.6998      R-sq = 20.5%      R-sq(adj) = 19.4%

Analysis of Variance

SOURCE        DF          SS          MS        •F          p
Regression     3      27.7123      9.2374      18.86      0.000
Error        220     107.7505      0.4898
Total        223     135.4628
```

An assumption of the multiple linear regression is that the residuals are normally distributed. This assumption should be verified by constructing a normal quantile plot with the **NSCOres** and **PLOT** commands for the residuals that were stored in C10.

The above output provides the estimated regression coefficients; $b_0 = 2.5899$, $b_1 = 0.16857$, $b_2 = 0.03432$, $b_3 = 0.04510$. These values are rounded and presented in the regression equation.

```
gpa = 2.59 + 0.169 hsm + 0.0343 hss + 0.0451 hse
```

The estimate of σ is given as $s = 0.6998$. The estimate is calculated as

$$s = \sqrt{\frac{\Sigma e_i^2}{n - p - 1}}$$

where the e_i's are the residuals and p is the number of predictor variables. In the column marked Stdev are the estimated standard errors: $s_{b_0} = 0.2942$, $s_{b_1} = 0.03549$, $s_{b_2} = 0.03756$, and $s_{b_3} = 0.03870$. A level C confidence interval for β_j can be computed as

$$b_j \pm t^* s_{b_j}$$

where t^* is the upper $(1 - C)/2$ critical value for the $t(n - p - 1)$ distribution. This is exactly the same as for simple linear regression. In that case, $p = 1$, so the number of degrees of freedom is $n - 2$.

To test the hypothesis $H_0 : \beta_j = 0$, the value of t is computed as

$$\frac{b_j}{s_{b_j}}$$

For each coefficient, the value appears in the column marked t-ratio. The values are given as 8.80, 4.75, 0.91, and 1.17. The *P*-values for a test against $H_a: \beta_j \neq 0$ are provided in the column marked p and are from the $t(n - p - 1)$ distribution.

The analysis of variance table for multiple regression is illustrated below. It has the same format as for simple linear regression. The only difference is that the number of degrees of freedom for the model increases from 1 to p, reflecting the fact that there are p explanatory variables. Similarly, the number of degrees of freedom for the error decreases from $n - 2$ to $n - p - 1$.

Analysis of Variance

SOURCE	DF	SS	MS	F	p
Regression	p	$\Sigma(\hat{y}_i - \bar{y})^2$	MSM=SSM/DFM	MSM/MSE	
Error	$n - p - 1$	$\Sigma(y_i - \hat{y}_i)^2$	MSE=SSE/DFE		
Total	$n - 1$	$\Sigma(y_i - \bar{y})^2$	MST=SST/DFT		

The value of MSE is the estimate of σ^2. In the example above, it is given as 0.4898. This value could also be obtained by squaring the estimate of σ ($s = 0.6998$). The ratio MSM/MSE is an *F* statistic for testing the null hypothesis

$$H_0: \beta_1 = \beta_2 = \cdots = \beta_p = 0$$

against the alternative hypothesis

$$H_a: \beta_j \neq 0 \text{ for at least one } j = 1, 2, \ldots, p$$

The test statistic has the $F(p, n - p - 1)$ distribution. In the example above, $F=18.86$. The *P*-value listed under the column marked p is given as 0.000. This means that there is strong evidence that at least one $\beta_j \neq 0$.

The value of R-sq is listed above as 20.5%. This means that the proportion of the variation in GPA that is explained by the HSM, HSS, and HSE scores is

$$R^2 = \frac{\text{SSM}}{\text{SST}} = 0.205$$

EXERCISES

9.1 Manatees are large sea creatures that live in the shallow water along the coast of Florida. Many manatees are injured or killed each year by powerboats. Below and in MANATEE.MTW are data on manatees killed and powerboat registrations (in thousands of boats) in Florida for the period 1977 to 1990.

Year	PowerBoat registrations	Manatees killed
1977	447	13
1978	460	21
1979	481	24
1980	498	16
1981	513	24
1982	512	20
1983	526	15
1984	559	34
1985	585	33
1986	614	33
1987	645	39
1988	675	43
1989	711	50
1990	719	47

(a)   Make a **PLOT** of boats registered versus manatees killed. Is there a strong straight-line pattern? What is the **CORRelation** for these data? Find the least-squares **REGRession** line. Draw this line on your scatterplot.

(b)   Is there strong evidence that the mean number of manatees killed increases as the number of powerboats increases? (State this question as null and alternative hypotheses about the slope of the population regression line, obtain the t statistic, and give your conclusion.)

(c)   Suppose that Florida were to restrict the number of powerboats to 700,000. How many manatees per year would be killed on the average if only 700,000 powerboats were allowed? Use the **PREDict** subcommand to give both a point prediction and a suitable 95% confidence or prediction interval.

9.3   The Leaning Tower of Pisa is an architectural wonder. Engineers concerned about the tower's stability have done extensive studies of its increasing tilt. Measurements of the lean of the tower over time provide much useful information. The following table gives measurements for the years 1975 to 1987. The variable "lean" represents the difference between where a point on the tower should be if the tower was straight and where it actually is. The data below and in PISA.MTW are coded as tenths of a millimeter in excess of 2.9 meters, so that the 1975 lean, which was 2.9642 meters, appears in the table as 642. (Data from G. Geri and B. Palla, "Considerazioni sulle più recenti osservazioni ottiche alla Torre Pendente di Pisa," *Estratto dal Bollettino della Società Italiana di Topografia e Fotogrammetria*, 2 (1988), pp. 121-135. Professor Julia Mortera of the University of Rome provided valuable assistance with the translation.)

Year	75	76	77	78	79	80	81	82	83	84	85	86	87
Lean	642	644	656	667	673	688	696	698	713	717	725	742	757

(a) **PLOT** the data. Does the trend in lean over time appear to be linear?

(b) What is the equation of the least-squares **REGRession** line? What percent of the variation in lean is explained by this line?

(c) Give a 95% confidence interval for the average rate of change (tenths of a millimeter per year) of the lean.

(d) In 1918 the lean was 2.9071 meters. (The coded value is 71.) Use the **PREDict** subcommand to calculate a predicted value for the lean in 1918. (Note that you must use the coded value 18 for year.) Although the least-squares line gives an excellent fit to the data for 1975 to 1987, this pattern did not extend back to 1918. Write a short statement explaining why this conclusion follows from the information available. Use numerical and graphical summaries to support your explanation.

(e) The engineers studying the Leaning Tower of Pisa are most interested in what will happen to the tower in the future. **PREDict** the tower's lean in the year 1997. To give a margin of error for the lean in 1997, would you use a confidence interval for a mean response or a prediction interval? Explain your choice.

9.6 Are ticket prices for professional basketball games related to the team's attendance? One way to address this question is to look at data on ticket prices and attendance for the 27 teams in the National Basketball Association. The data for the average ticket price (in dollars) and average paid attendance for the 1989-1990 NBA season are given in NBA.MTW and page 678 of *I.P.S.* (The data are from an article in the *Lafayette Journal and Courier*, June 26, 1990.)

(a) Find the least-squares **REGRession** line. What percent of the variation in attendance is explained by ticket price?

(b) Is linear regression on price of any value in explaining attendance? State hypotheses, report the test statistic and its *P*-value from the output, and state your conclusion.

(c) **PLOT** the data. In recent years, four new teams were added to the NBA. They are Charlotte, Miami, Minnesota, and Orlando. Circle the points corresponding to these teams on your plot and write the name of the team next to each of the circled points. Are any of the expansion teams outliers or influential points? Which ones?

(d) Redo the regression analysis omitting the data for Charlotte and Minnesota. How do the results of this analysis differ from (a) and (b)?

(e) Suppose that you are the general manager of an NBA team. You are considering raising the price of your tickets. On the basis of the analyses should you increase the price of your tickets? Suggest some lurking variables that might influence the average attendance at NBA basketball games for different teams.

9.16 FLOW.MTW gives data for a study of two methods for measuring the blood flow in the stomachs of dogs as follows.

Spheres	4.0	4.7	6.3	8.2	12.0	15.9	17.4	18.1	20.2	23.9
Vein	3.3	8.3	4.5	9.3	10.7	16.4	15.4	17.6	21.0	21.7

"Spheres" is an experimental method that the researchers hope will predict "vein," the standard but difficult method.

(a) Make a **PLOT** of spheres versus vein. Is there a strong straight-line pattern? What is the **CORRelation** for these data? Find the least-squares **REGRession** line. Draw this line on your scatterplot.

(b) We expect x and y to be positively associated. State hypotheses in terms of the slope of the population regression line that express this expectation, and carry out a significance test. What conclusion do you draw?

(c) Find a 99% confidence interval for the slope.

(d) Suppose that we observe a value of spheres equal to 15.0 for one specific dog. Give a 90% interval for predicting the variable vein.

9.17 POLLUTION.MTW gives data on air pollution measurements in two locations, rural and city. There are 26 cases for which both readings are present.

(a) Make a **PLOT** of the city reading versus the rural reading. Is there a strong straight-line pattern? What is the **CORRelation** for these data? Find the least-squares **REGRession** line. Draw this line on your scatterplot.

(b) State appropriate null and alternative hypotheses for assessing whether or not there is a linear relationship between the city and rural readings. Give the test statistic and report the P-value for testing your null hypothesis. Summarize your conclusion.

(c) The rural reading is 43 for a period during which the city equipment is out of service. Use the **PREDict** subcommand to find a 95% interval for the missing city reading.

9.18 Ohm's law, $I = V/R$, states that the current I in a metal wire is proportional to the voltage V applied to its ends and is inversely proportional to the resistance R in the wire. Students in a physics lab performed experiments to study Ohm's law. They varied the voltage and measured the current at each voltage with an ammeter. The goal was to determine the resistance R of the wire. We can rewrite Ohm's law in the form of a linear regression as $I = \beta_0 + \beta_1 V$, where $\beta_0 = 0$ and $\beta_1 = 1/R$. Because voltage is set by the experimenter, we think of V as the explanatory variable. The current I is the response. Below and stored in OHM.MTW are the data for one experiment. (Data provided by Sara McCabe.)

V	.50	1.00	1.50	1.80	2.0
I	.52	1.19	1.62	2.00	2.4

(a) **PLOT** the data. Are there any outliers or unusual points?

(b) Find the least-squares **REGRession** line to fit the data and estimate $1/R$ for this wire. Then give a 95% confidence interval for $1/R$.

(c)   If b_1 estimates $1/R$, then $1/b_1$ estimates R. Estimate the resistance R. Similarly, if L and U represent the lower and upper confidence limits for $1/R$, then the corresponding limits for R are given by $1/U$ and $1/L$, as long as L and U are positive. Use this fact and your answer to part (b) to find a 95% confidence interval for R.

(d)   State the null hypothesis tested by the ANOVA F statistic, and explain in plain language what this hypothesis says and give the P-value for the test of H_0.

(e)   Ohm's law states that b_0 in the model is 0. Calculate the test statistic for this hypothesis and give an approximate P-value.

(f)   Most statistical software systems have an option for doing regressions in which the intercept is set in advance to 0. In Minitab it is the **NOCOnstant** subcommand. Reanalyze the Ohm's law data given with this option and report the estimate of R. The output should also include an estimated standard error for $1/R$. Use this to calculate the 95% confidence interval for R. Note: With this option the degrees of freedom for t^* will be 1 greater than for the model with the intercept.

9.22   The human body takes in more oxygen when exercising than when it is at rest. To deliver the oxygen to the muscles, the heart must beat faster. Heart rate is easy to measure, but measuring oxygen uptake requires elaborate equipment. If oxygen uptake (VO2) can be accurately predicted from heart rate (HR) the predicted values can replace actually measured values for various research purposes. Unfortunately, not all human bodies are the same, so no single prediction equation works for all people. Researchers can, however, measure both HR and VO2 for one person under varying sets of exercise conditions and calculate a regression equation for predicting that person's oxygen uptake from heart rate. They can then use predicted oxygen uptakes in place of measured uptakes for this individual in later experiments. Below and in OXYGEN.MTW are data for one individual. (Data provided by Paul Waldsmith from experiments conducted in Don Corrigan's laboratory at Purdue University.)

HR	94	96	95	95	94	95	94	104	104	106
VO2	.473	.753	.929	.939	.832	.983	1.049	1.178	1.176	1.292

HR	108	110	113	113	118	115	121	127	131
VO2	1.403	1.499	1.529	1.599	1.749	1.746	1.897	2.040	2.231

(a)   **PLOT** the data. Are there any outliers or unusual points?

(b)   Compute the least-squares **REGRession** line for predicting oxygen uptake from heart rate for this individual.

(c)   Give the results from the test of the null hypothesis that the slope of the regression line is 0. Explain in words the meaning of your conclusion from this test.

(d)   Use the **PREDict** subcommand to calculate a 95% interval for the oxygen uptake of this individual on a future occasion when his heart rate is 95. Repeat the calculation for heart rate 110.

(e)   From what you have learned in (a), (b), (c), and (d) of this exercise, do you think that the researchers should use predicted VO2 in place of measured VO2 for this individual under similar experimental conditions? Explain your answer.

(f)   The data given were taken while the individual performed progressively more vigorous exercise. The observations are therefore in time order. In fact, the observations correspond to consecutive 1-minute periods. The statistical model for inference in linear regression assumes that the errors are independent and all have the same variance. **PLOT** the residuals versus the order in which the data were taken. Do you see any patterns that would lead you to question the validity of the regression methodology?

(g)   What null hypothesis is tested by the ANOVA F statistic? Give the P-value for the test of H_0.

(h)   Verify that the square of the t statistic is equal to the F statistic in your ANOVA table. (Any difference found is due to roundoff error.)

9.41   The following questions use the CSDATA.MTW worksheet described in the data appendix (page 792) of *I.P.S.*

(a)   Make a **PLOT** of GPA versus SATM. Do the same for GPA versus SATV. Describe the general patterns. Are there any unusual values?

(b)   Make a **PLOT** of GPA versus HSM. Do the same for the other two high school grade variables. Describe the three plots. Are there any outliers or influential points?

(c)   **REGRess** GPA on the three high school grade variables. Calculate and store the **RESIduals** from this regression. **PLOT** the residuals versus each of the three predictors and versus the predicted value of GPA. Are there any unusual points or patterns in these four plots?

(d)   Use the two SAT scores in a multiple **REGRession** to predict GPA. Calculate and store the residuals. **PLOT** the residuals versus each of the explanatory variables and versus the predicted GPA. Describe the plots.

9.45   It appears from Exercise 9.41 and the CSDATA.MTW worksheet that the mathematics explanatory variables are strong predictors of GPA in the computer science study.

(a)   Run a multiple regression using HSM and SATM to predict GPA. Give the fitted regression equation.

(b)   Report the value of the F statistic, its P-value, and your conclusion.

(c)   Give 95% confidence intervals for the regression coefficients of HSM and SATM. Do either of these include the point 0?

(d)   Report the t statistics and P-values for the tests of the regression coefficients of HSM and SATM. What conclusions do you draw from these tests?

(e)   What is the value of s, the estimate of σ?

(f)   What percent of the variation in GPA is explained by HSM and SATM in your model?

9.46 How well do verbal variables predict the performance of computer science students? Use the CSDATA.MTW worksheet to perform a multiple regression analysis to predict GPA from HSE and SATV. Summarize the results and compare them with those obtained in the previous exercise. In what ways do the regression results indicate that the mathematics variables are better predictors?

9.47 The WOOD.MTW worksheet contains two measurements of the strength of each of fifty strips of yellow poplar wood. The data set is described in the data appendix (page 792) of *I.P.S.* In this problem we look at this experiment as one in which the process of measuring strength is to be evaluated. Specifically, we ask how well a repeat measurement T2 can be predicted from the first measurement T1 for strips of wood of this type.
   (a)   **PLOT** T2 versus T1 and describe the pattern you see.
   (b)   Run the linear **REGRession** using T1 as the explanatory variable and T2 as the response variable. Write the fitted equation and give s, the estimate of the standard deviation σ of the model.
   (c)   What is the **CORRelation** between T1 and T2? This quantity is sometimes called the *reliability* of the strength-measuring procedure. What proportion of the variability in T2 is explained by T1?
   (d)   Use the **LET** command to find the t statistic for testing the null hypothesis that ρ is 0. State an appropriate alternative hypothesis for this problem and state the P-value for the significance test. Report your conclusions from parts (b), (c), and (d) in plain language.
   (e)   Verify that the square of the t statistic for the slope hypothesis is equal to the F statistic given in the ANOVA table.

9.48 Refer to the previous exercise and the WOOD.MTW worksheet. Rerun the regression for the 25 observations with odd-numbered strips; that is, $S = 1, 3, \ldots, 49$. We want to compare the results of this run with those for the full data set given in the previous exercise. In particular, we want to see which quantities remain approximately the same and which change.
   (a)   Construct a table giving b_0, b_1, s, and $s(b_1)$ for the two runs. Which values are approximately the same and which have changed?
   (b)   Summarize the differences between the two ANOVA tables.
   (c)   Compare the two correlations.
   (d)   Summarize your results in plain language. In particular, did your results in the previous exercise depend strongly on the quite large sample size?

9.49 This exercise uses the Gesell score data given in GESELL.MTW and the table below. Run a linear **REGRession** to predict Gesell score from age at first word. Use all 21 cases for this analysis and assume that the simple linear regression model holds.

Case	Age	Score	Case	Age	Score	Case	Age	Score
1	15	95	8	11	100	15	11	102
2	26	71	9	8	104	16	10	100
3	10	83	10	20	94	17	12	105
4	9	91	11	7	113	18	42	57
5	15	102	12	9	96	19	17	121
6	20	87	13	10	83	20	11	86
7	18	93	14	11	84	21	10	100

(a)   Write the fitted regression equation.

(b)   What is the value of the t statistic for testing the null hypothesis that the slope is 0? Give an approximate P-value for the test of H_0 versus the alternative that the slope is negative.

(c)   Give a 95% confidence interval for the slope.

(d)   What percentage of the variation in Gesell scores is explained by the age at first word?

(e)   What is s, the estimate of the model standard deviation σ?

(f)   Cases 18 and 19 in the Gesell data set were somewhat unusual. The simple linear regression model is therefore suspect when all cases are included. Rerun the analysis described in the previous exercise for this set of data with these two cases excluded. Compare your results with those obtained above. In particular, to what extent did the conclusions from the first regression run depend on these two cases?

9.51   Refer again to the CSDATA.MTW data set. The variable SEX has the value 1 for males and 2 for females. Create a data set containing the values for males only.

(a)   Run a multiple REGRession analysis for predicting GPA from the three high school grade variables for this group. Using the case study in *I.P.S.*, Section 9.2, as a guide, interpret the results, and state what conclusions can be drawn from this analysis. In what way (if any) do the results for males alone differ from those for all students?

(b)   Perform the analysis using the data for females only. Are there any important differences between female and male students in predicting GPA?

9.54   This exercise refers to the CHEESE.MTW described in the data appendix (page 791) of *I.P.S.* As cheddar cheese matures, a variety of chemical processes take place. The taste of mature cheese is related to the concentration of several chemicals in the final product. In a study of cheddar cheese from the LaTrobe Valley of Victoria, Australia, samples of cheese were analyzed for their chemical composition and were subjected to taste tests. The data are for one type of cheese manufacturing process. "Taste" is the response variable of interest. The taste scores were obtained by combining the scores from several tasters. Three of the chemicals whose concentrations were measured were acetic acid, hydrogen sulfide, and lactic acid. For acetic acid and hydrogen sulfide (natural) log transformations were taken. Thus the explanatory variables are the transformed concentrations of acetic acid ("acetic") and hydrogen sulfide ("H2S") and the untransformed concentration of lactic acid ("lactic"). (Data based on experiments performed by G. T. Lloyd and E. H. Ramshaw of the CSIRO Division of Food Research, Victoria, Australia. Some results of the statistical analyses of these data are given in G. McCabe, L. McCabe, and A. Miller, "Correlations and changes in flavour and chemical parameters of cheddar cheeses during maturation," *The Australian Journal of Dairy Technology*, 44 (1989), pp. 7-18.)

(a)   For each of the four variables, find the mean, median, standard deviation, and interquartile range. Display each distribution with a stemplot and use a normal quantile plot to assess normality of the data. Summarize your findings. Note that when doing regressions with these data, only the residuals from our model need be (approximately) normal.

(b)   Make a scatterplot for each pair of variables (you will have 6 plots). Describe the relationships. Calculate the correlation for each pair of variables and report the *P*-value for the test of zero population correlation in each case.

(c)   Perform a simple linear regression analysis using taste as the response variable and acetic as the explanatory variable. Be sure to examine the residuals carefully. Summarize your results. Include a plot of the data with the least-squares regression line. Plot the residuals versus each of the other two chemicals. Are any patterns evident? (These other chemicals are lurking variables for the simple linear regression.)

(d)   Repeat the analysis of (c) using taste as the response variable and H2S as the explanatory variable.

(e)   Repeat the analysis of (c) using taste as the response variable and lactic as the explanatory variable.

(f)   Compare the results of the regressions performed in (c), (d), and (e). Give a table with values of the *F* statistic, its *P*-value, R^2, and the estimate *s* of the standard deviation for each model. Report the three regression equations. Why are the intercepts in these three equations not all the same?

(g)   Carry out a multiple regression using acetic and H2S to predict taste. Summarize the results of your analysis. Compare the statistical significance of acetic in this model with its significance in the model with acetic alone as a predictor (c). Which model do you prefer? Give a simple explanation for the fact that acetic alone appears to be a good predictor of taste but with H2S in the model, it is not.

(h)   Carry out a multiple regression using H2S and lactic to predict taste. Comparing the results of this analysis to the simple linear regressions using each of these explanatory variables alone, it is evident that a better result is obtained by using both predictors in a model. Support this statement with explicit information obtained from your analysis.

(i)   Use the three explanatory variables acetic, H2S, and lactic in a multiple regression to predict taste. Write a short summary of your results including an examination of the residuals. Based on the regression analyses, which model do you prefer and why?

Chapter 10
Analysis of Variance

Commands to be covered in this chapter:

```
AOVOneway on the data in C...C
ONEWayaov data in C, subscripts in C
TABLe the data classified by C,...,C
TWOWayaov data in C, rows in C, columns in C
```

The AOVOneway Command

The **AOVOneway** command does one-way analysis of variance with the data for each level in a separate column. There must be two or more levels (columns) specified. The same number of observations is not required in each column. The command format is given below.

```
AOVOneway on the data in C...C
```

The command is demonstrated on data from Example 10.6 of *I.P.S.* In this example, three methods of instruction were compared in a study on reading comprehension. The three methods are called basal, DRTA, and strategies. The test scores for 22 students in each group are stored in a Minitab worksheet PRETEST.MTW.

```
MTB > info

COLUMN      NAME      COUNT
C1          Basal      22
C2          DRTA       22
C3          Strat      22

CONSTANTS USED: NONE
```

Before proceeding with the **AOVOneway** command, it is important to check that the assumptions of one-way analysis of variance are satisfied. Specifically, the populations are normal with possibly different means and the same variance. **BOXPlots** are useful for visually checking these assumptions. In addition, use the **NSCOres** and **PLOT** command to check for extreme deviations from normality. Compute the ratio of the largest to the smallest sample standard deviation as below.

```
MTB > desc c1-c3

                N      MEAN    MEDIAN    TRMEAN     STDEV    SEMEAN
Basal          22    10.500    11.500    10.550     2.972     0.634
DRTA           22     9.727     9.000     9.600     2.694     0.574
Strat          22     9.136     8.500     9.150     3.342     0.713

               MIN       MAX        Q1        Q3
Basal        4.000    16.000     8.000    12.000
DRTA         6.000    16.000     8.000    12.000
Strat        4.000    14.000     6.000    12.250

MTB > let k1 = std(c3)/std(c2)
MTB > print k1
K1         1.24084
```

Since the ratio of the largest to the smallest standard deviation is less than 2 and assuming that the normal quantile plots were satisfactory, the **AOVOneway** command can be used.

```
MTB > aovoneway c1 c2 c3

ANALYSIS OF VARIANCE
SOURCE      DF        SS        MS        F        p
FACTOR       2     20.58     10.29     1.13    0.329
ERROR       63    572.45      9.09
TOTAL       65    593.03
                                   INDIVIDUAL 95 PCT CI'S FOR MEAN
                                   BASED ON POOLED STDEV
  LEVEL      N      MEAN     STDEV   -----+---------+---------+---------+-
Basal       22    10.500     2.972              (---------*----------)
DRTA        22     9.727     2.694        (----------*----------)
Strat       22     9.136     3.342   (----------*----------)
                                   -----+---------+---------+---------+-
POOLED STDEV =     3.014         8.4       9.6      10.8      12.0
```

The output provides the ANOVA table. The columns in this table are labeled SOURCE, DF (degrees of freedom), SS (sum of squares), MS (mean square), F, and p. The rows in the table are labeled FACTOR, ERROR, and TOTAL. Consider our model

$$DATA = FIT + RESIDUAL$$

The FACTOR row corresponds to the FIT term, the ERROR row corresponds to the RESIDUAL term, and the TOTAL row corresponds to the DATA term. Notice that both the degrees of freedom and the sum of squares add to the value in the TOTAL row.

The output provides the pooled variance in the last line. It is given as equal to 3.014. Note that it can also be computed from the ANOVA table using the sum of squares and degrees of freedom for the ERROR row. That is,

$$s_p^2 = \frac{SS}{DF} = \frac{527.45}{64} = 9.0865$$

which implies that $s_p = 3.014$.

The F statistic is given in the ANOVA table. The null hypothesis being tested is

$$H_0: \mu_B = \mu_D = \mu_S$$

If H_0 is true, the F statistic has an $F(DFG, DFE)$ distribution, where DFG stands for degrees of freedom for groups and DFE stands for degrees of freedom for error. $DFG = I - 1$, the number of groups minus 1. $DFE = N - I$, the number of observations minus the number of groups. The P-value for this distribution is also given above. In this example, the P-value is 0.329 so we do not have evidence to reject H_0. For information purposes, the output from the **AOVOneway** command provides the mean and standard deviation for each group and plots individual 95% confidence intervals for the means. Each confidence interval is of the form

$$\left(\bar{x}_i - t \frac{s_p}{\sqrt{n_i}}, \bar{x}_i + t \frac{s_p}{\sqrt{n_i}} \right)$$

where $\bar{x}_i$ and n_i are the sample mean and sample size for level i, s_p = POOLED STDEV is the pooled estimate of the common standard deviation, and t^* is the value from a t table corresponding to 95% confidence and the degrees of freedom associated with MS ERROR.

The **ONEWayaov** Command

The command **ONEWayaov** does exactly the same analysis as **AOVOneway**, but uses a different form of input. The command format is given below.

```
ONEWayaov data in C, subscripts in C
```

The **ONEWayaov** command expects the data for all groups to be in a single column (the groups can be mixed together). A second column gives subscripts to say what group each observation belongs to. Subscripts should be integers between −10,000 and +10,000 or missing values (*). They need not be consecutive.

Data are often entered in the format required by the **ONEWayaov** command. The pretest scores are stored in READING.MTW in the column named 'PRE1' and the teaching methods are identified in a column named 'GROUP'. Group 1 corresponds to the Basal group, group 2 to the DRTA group, and group 3 to the Strat group. Below we demonstrate the **ONEWayaov** command with the data in READING.MTW. The output is exactly the same as above except that the groups are labeled 1, 2, and 3 instead of Basal, DRTA, and Strat.

```
MTB > onew 'pre1' 'group'

ANALYSIS OF VARIANCE ON Pre1
SOURCE       DF        SS        MS        F         p
Group         2     20.58     10.29     1.13     0.329
ERROR        63    572.45      9.09
TOTAL        65    593.03
                                        INDIVIDUAL 95 PCT CI'S FOR MEAN
                                        BASED ON POOLED STDEV
  LEVEL       N      MEAN     STDEV    -----+---------+---------+---------+-
      1      22    10.500     2.972                    (---------*----------)
      2      22     9.727     2.694             (----------*----------)
      3      22     9.136     3.342    (----------*----------)
                                        -----+---------+---------+---------+-
POOLED STDEV =       3.014             8.4       9.6      10.8      12.0
```

The TWOWayaov Command

The **TWOWayaov** command is used to compare the means of populations that are classified according to two factors. The command format for **TWOWayaov** is

```
TWOWayaov data in C, rows in C, columns in C
```

To use the **TWOWayaov** command, the design must be balanced, that is, each cell must contain the same number of observations. The **TABLe** command can be used to check that the design is balanced and to provide a preliminary analysis of the means and standard deviations. The **TABLe** command was introduced in Chapter 2 and has the following format.

```
TABLe the data classified by C,...,C
```

The command displays one-way, two-way, and multi-way tables. The cells may contain counts, percents, and summary statistics of associated variables (that is, any variable which is not used as a classification variable).

The **TABLe** command and two-way analysis of variance will be demonstrated on data found in MAJORS.MTW. The data come from a computer science study undertaken when it was noticed that many freshman computer science majors did not continue in this field of study. The data contain information about sex, final major, SAT scores, high school grades (math, English, and science), and college GPA. The variable names can be obtained from the **INFOrmation** command.

```
MTB > info

COLUMN       NAME        COUNT
C1           SEX          234
C2           MAJOR        234
C3           SATM         234
C4           SATV         234
C5           HSM          234
C6           HSE          234
C7           HSS          234
C8           GPA          234

CONSTANTS USED: NONE
```

Below we illustrate the **TABLe** command as described above.

```
MTB > table c1 c2;
SUBC> count;
SUBC> mean c8;
SUBC> std c8.


   ROWS: SEX      COLUMNS: MAJOR

                1           2           3         ALL

      1        39          39          39         117
            4.7474      5.0964      4.0477      4.6305
            0.6840      0.5130      0.7304      0.7785

      2        39          39          39         117
            4.9792      5.0808      4.5236      4.8612
            0.5335      0.6481      0.7656      0.6943

    ALL        78          78          78         234
            4.8633      5.0886      4.2856      4.7459
            0.6204      0.5807      0.7809      0.7450

   CELL CONTENTS --
                    COUNT
                gpa:MEAN
                    STD DEV
```

The counts indicate that there are 39 observations in each cell, so the design is balanced as required by the **TWOWayaov** command. The means should be plotted to examine differences between groups and to check for interactions. For example, below we compare the mean GPAs for male and female students. We use the **MPLOt** command to plot the GPA versus major for males and females on the same axes. This command is described in Chapter 2.

```
MTB > set c11
DATA> 1 2 3
DATA> set c12
DATA> 4.7474 5.0964 4.0477
DATA> set c13
DATA> 4.9792 5.0808 4.5236
DATA> end
```

```
MTB > name c11 'maj'
MTB > name c12 'gpa-m'
MTB > name c13 'gpa-f'
MTB > mplot c12 c11 c13 c11;
SUBC> xinc 1.
```

```
        -                              2
        -
        -            B
    4.90+
        -
        -            A
        -
        -
    4.55+                                          B
        -
        -
        -
        -
    4.20+
        -
        -                                          A
        -
        +---------+---------+---------+---------+---------+------
       0.0       1.0       2.0       3.0       4.0       5.0
          A = gpa-m vs. major     B = gpa-f vs. major
```

As with the one-way analysis of variance, the populations are assumed to be normal with possibly different means and the same variance. Normal quantile plots should be constructed using the **NSCOres** and **PLOT** commands to verify that the normal assumption is satisfied. Below we illustrate the use of the **TWOWayaov** command.

```
MTB > twow c8 c1 c2

ANALYSIS OF VARIANCE   gpa

SOURCE          DF          SS          MS
SEX              1        3.113       3.113
MAJOR            2       26.759      13.380
INTERACTION      2        2.356       1.178
ERROR          228       97.099       0.426
TOTAL          233      129.326
```

The **TWOWayaov** results are summarized in an ANOVA table printing the SOURCE, DF, SS, and MS columns for the main effects (SEX and MAJOR), the INTERACTION, the ERROR, and the TOTAL rows. To test for significance of the main effects and the interaction we use the F statistic. This is computed as the ratio of the mean square for SEX, MAJOR, or INTERACTION to the mean square ERROR. That is,

$$F_A = \frac{\text{MSA}}{\text{MSE}}, \quad F_B = \frac{\text{MSB}}{\text{MSE}}, \quad \text{and} \quad F_{AB} = \frac{\text{MSAB}}{\text{MSE}}$$

The values of these statistics are computed using the **LET** command. The P-values are then computed using the **CDF** command specifying the F distribution with the correct number of degrees of freedom in the subcommand. Since the `CDF` command computes $P(F < x)$, the *P*-value is equal to 1 minus the probability that is printed.

```
MTB > let k1 = 3.113/.426
MTB > cdf k1;
SUBC> f 1 228.
     7.3075    0.9926
MTB > let k2 = 13.380/.426
MTB > cdf k2;
SUBC> f 2 228.
    31.4085    1.0000
MTB > let k3 = 1.178/.426
MTB > cdf k3;
SUBC> f 2 228.
     2.7653    0.9349
```

The corresponding *P*-values are 0.0074, less than 0.0001, and 0.0665. That is, both main effects and the interaction are statistically significant.

EXERCISES

10.25   An experiment was conducted to assess the effects of nematodes on the growth of tomato seedlings. There were four treatments corresponding to 0, 1000, 5000, and 10,000 nematodes per plant. Each treatment was applied to four plants and the growth of the plants was recorded. The raw data appear in TOMATO.MTW and in the following table.

Nematodes	Seedling growth			
0	10.8	9.1	13.5	9.2
1000	11.1	11.1	8.2	11.3
5000	5.4	4.6	7.4	5.0
10,000	5.8	5.3	3.2	7.5

(a)   Use the `DESCribe` command with the `BY` subcommand to make a table of means and standard deviations for the four treatments.

(b)   State H_0 and H_a for an ANOVA on these data.

(c)   Use the `ONEWayaov` command on these data. What are the *F* statistic and its *P*-value? Give the values of s_p and R^2. Report your conclusion.

10.26   An experiment was conducted on the attractiveness of different colors to cereal leaf beetles. Four colors were tested, and six traps were used for each color. The raw data are given in the following table and COLOR.MTW.

Color	Insects trapped					
Lemon yellow	45	59	48	46	38	47
White	21	12	14	17	13	17
Green	37	32	15	25	39	41
Blue	16	11	20	21	14	7

(a)   Use the **DESCribe** command to make a table of means and standard deviations for the four colors.

(b)   State H_0 and H_a for an ANOVA on these data.

(c)   Using the **AOVOneway** command, run the ANOVA. What are the F statistic and its P-value? Do you reject H_0? Give the values of s_p and R^2.

10.45   An experiment was conducted to compare three methods of teaching reading. In the study there were two pretest and three posttest measures. The data are given in the READING.MTW data set described in the data appendix of *I.P.S.* (page 794). We have coded the groups as 1, 2, and 3 instead of Basal, DRTA, and Strat. For this exercise, use the data for the pretest variable PRE2.

(a)   Summarize the data using the **DESCribe** command with the **BY** subcommand to give the sample sizes, means, and standard deviations.

(b)   Examine the distribution of the scores in the three groups using the **NSCOres** and **PLOT** commands. Do the data look normal?

(c)   Use the **LET** command to find the ratio of the largest to the smallest standard deviation. Is it reasonable to proceed with the ANOVA?

(d)   Use the **ONEWayaov** command on these data. State H_0 and H_a for the ANOVA significance test. Report the value of the F statistic and its P-value. Do you have strong evidence against H_0?

(e)   Summarize your conclusions from this analysis.

10.46   Use the READING.MTW data to examine the effect on the ANOVA of changing the means. Use the pretest variable PRE2 for this exercise. Recall that we have coded the groups as 1, 2, and 3 instead of Basal, DRTA, and Strat. For each of the observations in the Basal group add one point to the PRE2. For each of the observations in the Strat group, subtract one point. Leave the observations in the DRTA group unchanged. Call the new variable PRE2X.

(a)   Summarize the PRE2X data using the **DESCribe** command with the **BY** subcommand to give the sample sizes, means, and standard deviations.

(b)   Use the **ONEWayaov** command on the variable PRE2X.

(c)   Compare the results of this analysis with the ANOVA for PRE2.

(d)   Summarize your conclusions.

10.47   For this exercise you will analyze the first posttest variable, given as POST1 in the READING.MTW data set.

(a)   Summarize the data using the **DESCribe** command with the **BY** subcommand to give the sample sizes, means, and standard deviations.

(b)   Examine the distribution of the scores in the three groups using the **NSCOres** and **PLOT** commands. Do the data look normal?

(c)   Use the **LET** command to compute the ratio of the largest to the smallest standard deviation. Is it reasonable to proceed with the ANOVA?

(d)   Use the **ONEWayaov** command and summarize the results.

10.48 For this exercise you will analyze the second posttest variable, given as POST2 in the READING.MTW data set.

    (a) Summarize the data using the **DESCribe** command with the **BY** subcommand to give the sample sizes, means, and standard deviations.

    (b) Examine the distribution of the scores in the three groups using the **NSCOres** and **PLOT** commands. Do the data look normal?

    (c) Use the **LET** command to compute the ratio of the largest to the smallest standard deviation. Is it reasonable to proceed with the ANOVA?

    (d) Use the **ONEWayaov** command and summarize the results.

10.49 Refer to the nematode experiment described in Exercise 10.25. Suppose that when entering TOMATO.MTW into the computer, you accidentally entered the first observation as 108 rather than 10.8. Use the **LET** command to change the appropriate value.

    (a) Use the **ONEWayaov** command with the incorrect observation. Summarize the results.

    (b) Compare this run with the results obtained with the correct data set. What does this illustrate about the effect of outliers in an ANOVA?

    (c) Summarize the data using the **DESCribe** command with the **BY** subcommand to give the sample sizes, means, and standard deviations for each of the four treatments using the incorrect data. How would this have helped you to detect the incorrect observation?

10.50 Refer to the color attractiveness experiment described in Exercise 10.26. Suppose that when entering COLOR.MTW into the computer, you accidentally entered the first observation as 450 rather than 45.

    (a) Use the **AOVOneway** command with the incorrect observation. Summarize the results.

    (b) Compare this run with the results obtained with the correct data set. What does this illustrate about the effect of outliers in an ANOVA?

    (c) Summarize the data using the **DESCribe** command with the **BY** subcommand to give the sample sizes, means, and standard deviations for each of the four treatments using the incorrect data. How would this have helped you to detect the incorrect observation?

10.51 Refer to the nematode experiment described in Exercise 10.25. With small numbers of observations in each group, it is often very difficult to detect deviations from normality and violations of the equal standard deviation assumption. The log transformation is often used for variables such as the growth of plants. In many cases this will tend to make the standard deviations more similar across groups and to make the data within each group look more normal. Transform the data in TOMATO.MTW using the **LET** or **LOGT** command. Rerun the **ONEWayaov** command using the logarithms of the recorded values. Answer the questions given in Exercise 10.25. Compare these results to those obtained by analyzing the raw data.

10.52   Refer to the color attractiveness experiment described in Exercise 10.26. The square root transformation is often used for variables that are counts, such as the number of insects trapped in this example. In many cases data transformed in this way will conform more closely to the assumptions of normality and equal standard deviations. Transform the data in COLOR.MTW using the **LET** or **SQRT** command. Rerun the **AOVOneway** command using the square roots of the original counts of insects. Answer the questions given in Exercise 10.26. Compare these results to those obtained by analyzing the raw data.

10.55   A large research project studied the physical properties of wood materials that were constructed by bonding together small flakes of wood. Different species of trees were used, and the flakes were made of different sizes. One of the physical properties measured was the tension modulus of elasticity in the direction perpendicular to the alignment of the flakes. The tension modulus of elasticity is measured in pounds per square inch (psi) and some of the data are given in the following table and in TENSION.MTW. The size of the flakes are $S1 = 0.015$ inches by 2 inches and $S2 = 0.025$ inches by 2 inches. (Data provided by Mike Hunt and Bob Lattanzi of the Purdue University Forestry Department.)

	Size of flakes	
Species	S1	S2
Aspen	308	278
	428	398
	426	331
Birch	214	534
	433	512
	231	320
Maple	272	158
	376	503
	322	220

(a)   Use the **TABLe** command with the **MEAN** and **STD** subcommands to compute means and standard deviations for the three observations in each species and size group. The **TABLe** command wil display both the means and the marginal means in a table.

(b)   Use the **MPLOt** command to plot the means of the six groups. Put species on the x axis and modulus of elasticity on the y axis. For each size connect the three points corresponding to the different species. Describe the patterns you see. Do the species appear to be different? What about the sizes? Does there appear to be an interaction?

(c)   Use the **TWOWayaov** command on these data. Use the **LET** and **CDF** commands to find the P-values for the main effects and the interaction. Summarize the results of the significance tests. What do these results say about the impressions that you described in part (b) of this exercise?

10.57 Use the data for the computer science study given in MAJORS.MTW. The data is described in the data appendix (page 795) of *I.P.S.* Analyze the data for SAT-V, the SAT verbal score. Your analysis should include a table of sample sizes, means, and standard deviations; normal quantile plots; a plot of the means; and a two-way ANOVA using sex and major as the factors. Write a short summary of your conclusions.

10.58 Use the data for the computer science study given in MAJORS.MTW. Analyze the data for HSS, the high school science grades. Your analysis should include a table of sample sizes, means, and standard deviations; normal quantile plots; a plot of the means; and a two-way ANOVA using sex and major as the factors. Write a short summary of your conclusions.

10.59 Use the data for the computer science study given in MAJORS.MTW. Analyze the data for HSE, the high school English grades. Your analysis should include a table of sample sizes, means, and standard deviations; normal quantile plots; a plot of the means; and a two-way ANOVA using sex and major as the factors. Write a short summary of your conclusions.

10.60 Use the data for the computer science study given in MAJORS.MTW. Analyze the data for GPA, the college grade point average. Your analysis should include a table of sample sizes, means, and standard deviations; normal quantile plots; a plot of the means; and a two-way ANOVA using sex and major as the factors. Write a short summary of your conclusions.

Appendix
List of Minitab Commands and Subcommands
(Subcommands are shown indented under the main command.)

Notation:

K   denotes a constant such as 8.3 or k14

C   denotes a column, such as C12 or 'Height'

E   denotes either a constant or column

[ ]   encloses an optional argument

1. General Information

HELP [command] [subcommand]

INFOrmation [on C,...,C] on status of worksheet

STOP session

2. Input and Output of Data

READ the following data into C,...,C

SET the following data into C

INSErt data [between rows K and K] of C,...,C

END of data

NAME C is 'NAME', C is 'NAME',...,C is 'NAME'

PRINt E,...,E

SAVE [in 'FILENAME'] a copy of the worksheet

RETRieve the saved Minitab worksheet from 'FILENAME'

3. Editing and Manipulating Data

LET C(K) = K

DELEte rows K,...,K of C,...,C

ERASe E,...,E

INSErt data [betwen rows K and K] of C,...,C

CODE (K...K) to K...(K...K) to K for C...C, store in C...C

STACk (E,...,E) on ... on (E,...,E), put into (C,...,C)

     SUBScripts into C

UNSTack (C,...,C) into (E,...,E),...,(E,...,E)
    SUBScripts are in C

SORT C [carry along C,...,C] put into C [and C,...,C]
    DESCending C,...,C

4.   Arithmetic

LET (algebraic expression, complete on one line)
    (Expressions may use arithmetic operators +, -, *, /, and ** (exponentiation),
    and any of the following: SQRT, LOGTen, LOGE, EXPO, ANTIlog,
    ROUNd, COUNt, N, SUM, MEAN, STDev, MEDIan, MINimum,
    MAXimum)

Simple Arithmetic Operations:

ADD E to E,...,to E, put into E

SUBTract E from E, put into E

MULTiply E by E,...,by E, put into E

DIVIde E by E, put into E

RAISe E to the power E, put into E

Columnwise Functions:

ABSOlute value of E, put into E

SQRT of E, put into E

LOGE of E, put into E

LOGTen of E, put into E

EXPOnentiate E, put into E

ANTIlog of E, put into E

ROUNd to integer E, put into E

Normal Scores:

NSCOres of C, put into C

Columnwise Statistics:

COUNt the number of values in C [put into K]

N (number of nonmissing values in) C [put into K]

NMISs (number of missing values in) C [put into K]

SUM of the values in C [put sum into K]

MEAN of values in C [put mean into K]

STDev of the values in C [put into K]

MEDIan of the values in C [put into K]

MINimum of the values in C [put into K]

MAXimum of the values in C [put into K]

SSQ (uncorrected sum of squares) for C [put into K]

Rowwise Statistics:

RCOUnt of E,...,E put into C

RN of E,...,E put into C

RNMIss of E,...,E put into C

RSUM of E,...,E put into C

RMEAn of E,...,E put mean of each row into C

RSTDev of E,...,E put into C

RMEDian of E,...,E put into C

RMINimum of E,...,E put into C

RMAXmum of E,...,E put into C

RSSQ of E,...,E put into C

5. Plotting Data

DOTPlot of data in C,...,C

    INCRement = K

    STARt at K [end at K]

    BY C

    SAME scales for all columns

HISTogram of C,...,C

    INCRement = K

    STARt at K [end at K]

    BY distinct values in C

    SAME scales for all columns

STEM-and-leaf display of C,...,C

    BY distinct values in C

BOXPlot for data in C

    BY distinct values in C

PLOT C vs C

    YINCrement = K

    YSTArt = K

    XINCrement = K

    XSTArt = K

MPLOt C vs C, and C vs C, and ,..., C vs C

    YINCrement = K

    YSTArt = K

    XINCrement = K

    XSTArt = K

LPLOt C vs C using labels as coded in C

    YINCrement = K

    YSTArt = K

    XINCrement = K

    XSTArt = K

TSPLot [period K] time series data in C

6. Basic Statistics

DESCribe the data in C,...,C

    BY C

ZINTerval [K% confidence] sigma = K, for C,...,C

ZTESt [of mu = K] assumed sigma = K on C,...,C

    ALTernative = K

TINTerval [with K percent confidence] for data in C,...,C

TTESt [of mu = K] on data in C,...,C

    ALTernative = K

STESt [of median = K] for data in C,...,C

    ALTernative = K

TWOSample t [K% confidence] for data in C and C

    ALTernative = K

    POOLed procedure

TWOT [K% confidence] for data in C, subscripts in C

    ALTernative = K

    POOLed procedure

CORRelate the data in C,...,C

7. Regression

REGRess C on K predictors C,...,C
    NOCOnstant
    RESIduals put into C
    PREDict for E,...,E
BRIEf K

8. Analysis of Variance

AOVOneway on the data in C,...,C
ONEWayaov data in C, subscripts in C
TWOWayaov data in C, rows in C, columns in C

9. Tables

TALLy the data in columns C,...,C
    COUNts
    PERCents
    CUMCounts cumulative counts
    CUMPercents cumulative percents
    ALL four statistics above
TABLe the data classified by C,...,C
    MEANs for C...C
    STDev for C,...,C
    COUNts
    ROWPercents
    COLPercents
    TOTPercents
    CHISquare test [output code = K]
CHISquare analysis on frequency table in C,...,C

10. Statistical Process Control

ICHArt for C,...,C
    MU = K
    SIGMa = K
    SLIMits are K,...,K
    TEST K,...,K

XBARchart for C,...,C, subgroups are in E
> **MU** = K
>
> **SIGMa** = K
>
> **SLIMits** are K,...,K
>
> **TEST** K,...,K

PCHArt, proportion nonconforming in C,...,C, sample size = E
> **P** = K
>
> **SLIMits** are K,...,K
>
> **TEST** K,...,K

11. Distributions and Random Data

RANDom K observations into each of C,...,C
> **BERNoulli** trials with p = K
>
> **BINOmial** n = K, p = K
>
> **DISCrete** dist. with values in C and probabilities in C
>
> **NORMal** [mu = K [sigma = K]]
>
> **UNIForm** [continuous on the interval K to K]

PDF for values in E [store results in E]
> **BINOmial** n = K, p = K

CDF for values in E [store results in E]
> **BINOmial** n = K, p = K
>
> **NORMal** [mu = K [sigma = K]]
>
> **T** with degrees of freedom = K
>
> **F** with df numerator = K, df denominator = K
>
> **CHISquare** with df = K

INVCdf for values in E [store results in E]
> **BINOmial** n = K, p = K
>
> **NORMal** [mu = K [sigma = K]]
>
> **T** with degrees of freedom = K
>
> **F** with df numerator = K, df denominator = K
>
> **CHISquare** with df = K

SAMPle K rows from C...C put into C...C

12. Miscellaneous

ERASe all data in E,...,E

OUTFile 'FILENAME'

NOOUtfile

BRIEf = [with output code = K] for commands that follow

13. Stored Commands and Loops

EXECute commands [in 'filename']

STORe [in 'filename']

NOTE any comments may be put here

END of storing commands

ECHO the commands that follow

NOECho the commands that follow

14. Symbols

*   Missing Value Symbol. An asterisks (*) can be used as data in **READ**, **SET** and **INSErt** and in datafiles. Enclose the asterisk in single quotes in commands and subcommands.

\#   Comment Symbol. The pound sign (#) anywhere on a line tells Minitab to ignore the rest of the line.

&   Continuation Symbol. To continue a command onto another line, end the first line with the ampersand (&). You can use ++ as a synonym for &.

Index

TO PRINT

MTB> paper
MTB> whatever it is you want
MTB> no paper

    ctrl "Z"

lpr ___ - Pstaracielabs___ PRINTER.us
     sp   ↑cap   sp ↑caps.

Remove

% rm PRINTER.us ← name of file

Are you sure — Y.

% lynx

  Go)to

www. math. yorku. ca / who / Faculty / Buttler /
    Math 1131 / 1131 - home. html.
  (list the List) ———→
P)rint → save to disk
  Call " Census. 1. dat"